JULIE GOODWIN'S
20$|20🕐 MEALS

JULIE GOODWIN'S
20$|20🕐 MEALS

FEED YOUR FAMILY FOR $20 IN 20 MINUTES

CONTENTS

TWENTY DOLLARS,
TWENTY MINUTES,
AND DINNER IS DONE!

20|20

INTRODUCTION

There are all different kinds of cooking, but in most households they mainly fall into two categories: the cooking that we choose to do, and the cooking that we have to do. The cooking I choose to do includes pottering around on a rainy day, making roasts or slow braises, baking or stirring or getting ready for a dinner party.

This book is about the cooking that we *have* to do – the day in, day out feeding of our families. It's about reducing the hassles and the cost and sharing some ideas that will keep everybody happy.

I sometimes hear people say that it's cheaper to buy takeaway than it is to make home-cooked meals with quality produce. I don't believe that, and in *20/20 Meals* I will demonstrate that it is absolutely possible to create beautiful meals for the family with a modest budget, without sacrificing freshness, quality or enjoyment.

20/20 Meals will make the daily task of cooking for the family a little easier. Using the ideas and recipes in this book, you can produce meals on time and to a budget.

'What's for dinner?' is the inevitable daily question, and coming up with an answer day in and day out is challenging. In this book, you will find plenty of ideas to keep everyone happy – tasty, fresh food, cooked from scratch, on time and to a budget. Twenty dollars, twenty minutes, and dinner is done!

Julie

GET SET FOR SUCCESS

Having a streamlined kitchen is the key to cooking efficiently. One of the biggest obstacles to getting dinner done on time is hunting around for elusive ingredients or utensils. When my kitchen benches, pantry or fridge become cluttered, it slows me down considerably, so I give them a bit of attention to streamline things again. The following areas need to be fairly organised if you want to have dinner on the table in 20 minutes.

BENCHES

I used to dream of the kind of kitchens you see in show homes, with wide expanses of gleaming bench and not a cooking implement in sight. I gave up on that some time ago. Mine is a working kitchen, and it looks like one. My benchtops hold the larger items of equipment I use regularly, like the food processor, electric mixer and of course a knife block. Getting things like that out of the cupboard is a hassle, and it just makes life easier if they're out and ready to go.

Beside the stovetop is a caddy that holds the things I use a lot in my cooking – a couple of types of oil, salt, pepper, cooking spray.

Just as important as having the things you need handy is getting rid of anything that doesn't belong. My benches seem to attract things like mail, school notes and occasionally sporting equipment or clothes. I have found that it's almost impossible to train my family not to dump things there, but I will never give up trying.

THE PANTRY

The pantry is one of the most important parts of the kitchen to have organised. I would highly recommend a pantry overhaul to anyone wanting to save time in the kitchen. I wish I could have back all the hours I've spent staring into a cluttered cupboard trying to locate an ingredient.

An organised pantry also saves money – when the shelves are clear and you know what's in there, you don't buy those ingredients again and end up with several half-empty bottles of the same sauce and out-of-date packets and jars.

I find that the best helpers in the pantry are shallow baskets or caddies, similar to the one I keep near the stovetop with my oil and salt. In the pantry I have dedicated caddies for different things. One has the items that go on the dinner table – salt and pepper grinders, sauce, toothpicks and serviettes. Hardly fine dining, I know, but it speeds up the process of setting and clearing the table each night.

Another caddy contains all my Asian pantry ingredients, like soy sauce, rice wine vinegar and sesame oil. This means if I am cooking an Asian-style dish I can either bring out that one caddy or easily find what I need.

Storing opened packets of food properly in airtight containers and snap-lock bags also saves a lot of waste by keeping food fresh. See-through canisters with sticky labels make identification easy. Things such as pasta, once opened, can be popped into a snap-lock bag rather than put away in the open packet, to keep it in top condition. (It's an unfortunate fact that about one-third of all food goes to waste. By keeping the kitchen organised and storing things properly, we can dramatically reduce the amount of waste produced in our own households, which saves money as well as being beneficial to our planet.)

Writing on the edge of the pantry shelves or putting stickers there helps other members of the family to put things away where they belong, too.

PANTRY ESSENTIALS

Keeping the pantry well-stocked is the key. A range of dried pastas, shelf-fresh noodles and rice provides a solid basis for hundreds of great meals. Tinned goods such as tomatoes, tuna and chickpeas are a helpful standby, too. I always have a variety of flavours in the form of dried herbs and spices, vinegars, condiments and oils. When the pantry is well stocked and organised, it's as easy as 1-2-3 to add some fresh protein and vegetables and get dinner on the table with no fuss at all.

THE SPICE RACK

A spice rack isn't quite big enough for my purposes. I have a drawer dedicated to dried herbs and spices. I found all those little jars and packets jammed up the pantry and got lost among other things. My spice drawer also has some little baskets in it, to keep things organised. It sounds awfully obsessive, but having things in alphabetical order helps me to lay my hands on what I need quickly. You may prefer to organise them by cuisine. It's really about setting up your cooking space in a way that makes sense to you.

THE FRIDGE

The fridge is the part of my kitchen that can get out of control most quickly. Regular clean-outs are important to make sure that food gets used instead

of wilting away at the back until it's inedible. Having a plan for leftovers is helpful – for instance, storing them in a lunch box ready for the next day.

I use little shallow baskets in the fridge as well, to keep jars in their categories – jams in one, condiments in another, curry pastes and sauces in a third. Once again it sounds a little obsessive, but I needed to do it after one clean-out yielded so many half-used jars of mustard and relish that I had to perform an intervention on myself and change my ways.

The veggie drawer needs regular attention so that wrinkled carrots and slimy greens don't take up residence. Planning menus ahead is useful here, as you won't buy things you don't need. Also, once again, good storage is key. Air and heat are the two biggest enemies of fresh produce, so airtight snap-lock bags are invaluable.

When the fridge is cluttered, it's harder to find things, so the door stays open longer. It also runs less efficiently and won't keep food at the correct temperature. Both of these things speed up the deterioration process and use more power than necessary, so an organised fridge saves time and money.

EQUIPMENT AND UTENSIL STORAGE

As you cook, identify the things that you use all the time, and give them their own space. For instance, I have a utensil drawer that only contains the things I use almost every time I cook – a couple of wooden spoons and spatulas, a peeler, cup and spoon measures and so on. There's a full list of all the equipment you'll need to cook from this book on page 9, but the key here is to find a new home for the utensils you don't use all that often (or ever).

Things like the turkey baster, candy thermometer, cookie cutters, that fancy little item that turns cucumbers into spaghetti – get them out of the utensil drawer and put them somewhere else. (If you haven't used them for a really long time, the 'somewhere else' might be a box to take to Vinnies.)

The same goes for the pots and pans drawer – the whole set doesn't have to be in one place. Keep the ones you use handy, and store the others out of the way. There's nothing worse than fighting a bunch of pots, pans and random lids to get your favourite one out.

You can apply this theory everywhere in the kitchen. Chopping boards, colanders, wraps and snap-lock bags, everything you need to prep, cook and store your food should have a home of its own. (I have managed to organise most of these areas, but admit to failure when it comes to the Tupperware drawer. If anyone can help me with that, I would be very grateful. Where, oh where do the lids go?)

EQUIPMENT ESSENTIALS

Below is a comprehensive list of all the equipment you will need to cook the recipes in *20/20 Meals*. They are grouped together in a logical way (to me, at least!) – electrical, cookware, measuring and mixing, large utensils, small utensils, consumables and serving ware.

To cook quickly and efficiently, there are some items in the kitchen I just can't do without. Of course you can create meals without a food processor or a hand-held stick mixer, but the process is much slower. For the recipes in this book to be achievable in 20 minutes, there is certain equipment I deem to be 'not negotiable'. Besides the equipment that most kitchens have, like an oven and microwave, these are the items I consider to be a great investment:

Food processor and mini food processor; hand-held stick mixer; chef pan (this is 30–38 cm across, is non-stick, has oven-proof handles and sides about 7 cm deep, and comes with a lid); a large pot, which will be about 30 cm across and deep enough to hold at least 4 litres of water, for cooking pasta; a microwave rice cooker, which is essentially a microwave-safe container with a tightly fitting lid; a set of good, sharp knives including a large chef knife; and of course all the little bits and pieces like a fine (zesting) grater, spoons and spatulas.

ELECTRICAL APPLIANCES:
Oven
Oven grill
Microwave
Food processor
Mini food processor
Toaster
Kettle
Hand-held stick mixer

COOKWARE:
Large pot with lid
Chef pan with lid
Medium pot
Wok
28 cm oven-proof non-stick
  frypan
Medium frypan
Baking dish
Baking tray
Grill plate
Microwave rice cooker

MEASURING:
Large measuring jug
Cup measures
Measuring spoons

MIXING:
Bowl
Mixing bowl, large
Mixing bowl, medium
Mixing bowl, small
Shallow dish
Narrow jug

LARGE UTENSILS:
Chopping board
Wire rack
Colander
Mandolin/V-slicer with plain
  and julienne attachments
Wire mesh strainer

SMALL UTENSILS:
Knife
Bread knife
Fine grater
Tin opener
Citrus squeezer
Spatula
Spoon
Big spoon
Large slotted spoon
Wooden spoon
Teaspoon
Tongs
Vegetable peeler
Egg flip
Garlic crusher
Ladle
Meat mallet
Pasta server
Pastry brush
Pizza cutter
Whisk
Timer
Grater
Kitchen scissors
Oven mitt
Long metal skewers
Fork

CONSUMABLES:
Baking paper
Foil
Paper towel
Plastic wrap
Snap-lock bags

SERVING WARE:
Salad bowl
Shallow pie or gratin dish
Ramekin
Noodle bowl
Dinner plates or platters
  (at least 28 cm in diameter)
Plate
Serving bowls
Serving platter

TIME TO COOK

Removing obstacles from the kitchen and setting everything up in a logical way is probably the biggest key to cooking quickly and efficiently. It's more important than having amazing knife skills or being the world's fastest potato peeler.

Not only the recipes in this book but your own tried-and-true stand-by recipes will be faster and easier if you get set for success. It's an effort, but well worth it, I promise.

Happy cooking!

SETTING UP EVERYTHING IN A LOGICAL
WAY IS PROBABLY THE BIGGEST KEY
TO COOKING QUICKLY AND EFFICIENTLY

20|20

HOW THE TIMING WORKS

The '20 minutes' part of the title of this book refers to preparation and cooking time. The time starts from when the ingredients and equipment are out on the bench. Not measured, or chopped, or heated, just out and ready to use.

THERE IS ONE EXCEPTION TO THIS, WHICH IS THE RECIPES WITH THE 'OVEN ON' SYMBOL – OR THE OVEN GRILL SYMBOL, WHICH HAS A WAVY LINE ABOVE THE ON SIGN. I COULDN'T BRING MYSELF TO RULE THE OVEN OUT OF THE BOOK ALTOGETHER, SO IF YOU ARE HOME IN TIME TO PREHEAT THE OVEN, FLICK IT ON FOR THOSE RECIPES. IF NOT, JUST CHOOSE ONE OF THE OTHERS.

Now, I know that getting things out to cook with takes time. But every household has a different level of organisation and I can't estimate how long it takes for people with cavernous pantries or chock-a-block fridges and cupboards to gather their things together. So I have started the time from when the items are gathered.

In this book are all my best tips for an efficient and streamlined working kitchen, which will dramatically reduce the time it takes to get things together. If you are committed to making the everyday job of cooking dinner easier and faster, I highly recommend following the steps set out in the 'Get set for success' pages. Even if you don't follow these steps, the recipes will still work in 20 minutes, once everything is out and ready, but you will spend far less time getting to that point if you do.

Some of the cooking methods in this book will seem slightly different to the usual. That's because cooking quickly and super-efficiently requires a different approach to the job. It's about high heat and economy of movement, rather than the therapeutic, gently simmering, stirring-slowly kind of dishes that I love to make when I have time for leisurely cooking.

There is an equipment list on page 9, and certain items on it are 'not negotiable'. These are necessary for the recipes to work in the allotted time. You can still cook the recipes without them, but it might take more than 20 minutes. There's no weird or wonderful gear there – they are standard items that many kitchens will already have.

You won't need clever knife skills to make the recipes in this book, either. Anything that needs to be finely chopped can be popped into a food processor. Meat is not sliced paper-thin and there's no fancy julienning of vegetables by hand. Those with only basic knife skills should still have success with these recipes.

I have avoided using pre-cut vegetables, as they are more expensive, have more packaging and deteriorate more quickly once cut. The one shortcut I do take is buying pre-grated cheese. It doesn't cost much more than a block, it doesn't deteriorate like cut vegetables do, and it saves a lot of time and hassle.

There are things you can do when shopping to make cooking faster as well, such as selecting a bunch of fat shallots rather than the little skinny ones that are more fiddly to peel.

One thing that slows me down when cooking is pausing to clean things I need to use a second time. For this reason, you'll often see 2 chopping boards and 2 knives on the equipment list. This means there's one ready to go for meat and another ready for vegetables, and you won't have to stop and wash up in between.

So in short – if you follow the recipe, it will be 20 minutes from the time you have your ingredients and gear out until you are enjoying your meal!

TIME-SAVING IDEAS

There are many time-saving tips outlined in the 'Get set for success' pages, but here are a few more.

> Spend a little bit of time after shopping to save time and effort down the track. Freeze meat in meal-sized portions and maybe pop a simple marinade into a snap-lock bag so it's ready to cook.

> Take your meat out of the freezer in the morning, to defrost in the fridge throughout the day.

> When setting up to cook, run a sink of hot soapy water. Pots and dishes can start to soak, saving cleaning time after the meal.

> When cooking, have a couple of containers on the bench – one for organic scraps and one for rubbish. This saves trips to and from the compost bucket and rubbish bin and keeps the workspace organised.

> Spend some time on Sunday night organising lunches, so you won't mess up the kitchen making them every morning.

> When you are making a slow-cooked meal like a braise or curry, double or triple the recipe and freeze the rest for another night.

> Shop for the whole week at once, so you won't need to make multiple trips to the shops.

> When buying bunches of shallots (also known as spring onions), buy fat rather than thin ones to reduce peeling time.

> To cut green beans quickly, line the tops up using your knife blade and do them all at once. The tails don't need to be removed if the beans are nice and fresh.

> There's no need to peel garlic cloves – just pop them in the crusher whole.

> Enlist help! Many hands make quick work.

HOW THE PRICING WORKS

This is a book about cooking to a budget, but it's not about doing things as cheaply as possible. You can buy quality, ethical, local food, and still do it inexpensively. Beautiful food, when made from scratch, does not need to be expensive.

Recently there has been a lot of discussion about how meals are priced and presented to consumers. Some methods assume that items in your pantry don't cost anything. Some believe that if you have to buy a jar of spice for $3.50, the whole jar should be part of the recipe cost.

The recipes in this book have been priced using the 'actual cost' method. Everything that has been bought has a cost ascribed to it, but only the amount used in the recipe is counted. Using the spice example, you wouldn't buy the jar, use a tablespoon and throw the rest away. I've calculated the cost of these recipes using the price of that tablespoon, rather than the price of the whole jar. Most ingredients in this book are used in more than one recipe, so it's unlikely that you'll buy an ingredient and waste the bulk of it.

Of course prices range dramatically from place to place and time to time, so I have tried to be as realistic as possible in keeping these recipes under $20. All ingredients are at full price, not on special. I did not use generic brands, unless that was all that was available.

I always buy Australian produce when it
is available, even when imports are cheaper,
as I believe in supporting our producers and
buying food with the smallest possible impact
on the environment.

The 'What's in season' chart beginning on page 220 is a valuable tool for keeping costs down. When fruit and vegetables are in season they are much cheaper and at their peak in flavour and nutrition. The fruit and vegetables in these recipes were priced in season.

Some items seem cheaper on the shelf, but have other costs attached. For example, cage eggs. They're a little cheaper per egg, but the cost to the chickens who lay them is tremendous. I pay the extra for free-range eggs and the recipes in this book are priced accordingly. There is plenty of labelling around now to direct us to ethically produced products – RSPCA-approved chicken, Australian sow stall free pork, Australian seafood. My pricing is based on these products, not their cheaper counterparts.

Wherever there is a serving suggestion, such as bread served on the side, it has also been priced and is covered by the $20 budget.

All of the recipes in this book are under $20. Some are well under. If you are a clever shopper and take advantage of bulk buys and specials, you can make them for even less!

Each recipe serves a family of four –
and if you're lucky there may be leftovers
for lunch the next day!

MONEY-SAVING IDEAS

Here are a few ways to save money in the kitchen by shopping smart and reducing waste.

> Fresh herbs add so much to a meal, but they perish quickly. If you are buying fresh herbs, plan the week's menu so they will all get used up. Storing them correctly in airtight snap-lock bags will help them keep a lot longer.

> It's even cheaper to grow your own. Live herbs in pots are barely more expensive than a cut bunch, and they can grow in amidst your other plants, or in pots, if you don't have space for a herb patch.

> Food storage is vitally important. Wasted food is wasted money. Getting fresh produce into the fridge should be a priority after shopping. Sealing opened packets of pantry items in airtight bags or canisters also helps to keep them from perishing.

> Buy in bulk and take advantage of bulk discounts. When buying bulk meat, divide it up into meal-sized portions before freezing.

> Plan ahead – going to the shops with a list will save on impulse buys.

> Buy in season. Seasonal fruit and vegetables are not only much nicer, they are much cheaper.

> If you are sending lunches to school with kids, little packets of snacks can be very costly. It is far less expensive to buy big packets of pretzels or dried fruit, or make your own popcorn, and divide them up into small snap-lock bags.

> When you have time for slow cooking, consider cheaper cuts of meat. Shin and gravy beef, lamb shank and neck, and chicken drumsticks are just some examples of meat that is very inexpensive but delicious when simmered away in a slow cooker.

> Cook in bulk and freeze for another day – this saves time, electricity and effort. Great foods for freezing include bolognese sauce, casseroles, braises and curries.

> Cook as much as you can from scratch. Processed foods are more expensive. Compare raw potatoes with frozen potatoes in a bag as an example.

> Bacon with the rind on is less expensive than rindless. The rind can be very quickly removed by pinching through it in the middle of the rasher and simply peeling it away.

> Develop a relationship with your butcher, fishmonger and greengrocer. They will help steer you towards the best buys if you ask.

> Don't throw away bruised or overripe fruit. It can be used in cakes, fritters or sauces.

> Put stale bread or crusts in the freezer. When you have enough, process them for homemade breadcrumbs. The breadcrumbs can be frozen for three months, too.

> Clean out the fridge often – an overloaded fridge uses more power. Check the seals regularly to make sure no cold air is escaping.

> Label foods before freezing them so that you use them within three months.

FASTER
THAN PASTA

THE SLOWEST THING ABOUT MAKING PASTA IS
USUALLY GETTING THE WATER TO BOIL! FOR MOST
OF THESE RECIPES YOU'LL NEED A LARGE POT WITH
A LID. MY PASTA POT IS 30 CM ACROSS AND 15 CM
DEEP AND IT DOES THE JOB NICELY. IF YOU FOLLOW
THE DIRECTIONS IN THE RECIPES, THE WATER COMES
UP TO THE BOIL NICE AND QUICKLY. AND BY THE
TIME THE PASTA IS COOKED, THE REST OF
THE MEAL WILL BE TOO!

I'VE ALSO INCLUDED NOODLE RECIPES IN THIS
CHAPTER. AND WITH SO MANY GLUTEN-FREE OPTIONS
READILY AVAILABLE NOW, THE WHOLE FAMILY CAN
ENJOY BEAUTIFUL PASTA DINNERS.

RECIPES

HONEY MUSTARD CHICKEN
WITH BROCCOLINI PASTA 52

SMOKED SALMON SPAGHETTI 55

VIETNAMESE-STYLE NOODLE SOUP 56

PASTA BOSCAIOLA 59

PAPPARDELLE WITH SPECK,
PEAS AND SHALLOTS 60

TUNA MORNAY 63

SWEET AND SOUR VEGGIE NOODLES 64

PORK PAD THAI 67

SPAGHETTI NAPOLITANA WITH ITALIAN SALAD 68

CHICKEN NOODLES WITH OYSTER SAUCE 71

CHICKEN CACCIATORE

INGREDIENTS

1 tablespoon cooking salt

375 g dried small spiral pasta

800 g chicken thigh fillets

¼ cup flour

1 tablespoon olive oil

2 garlic cloves

1 large brown onion

2 tablespoons tomato paste

1 teaspoon dried oregano leaves

800 g tin crushed tomatoes

½ teaspoon salt

½ teaspoon ground black pepper

½ cup red wine

About 20 pitted kalamata olives

½ bunch flat-leaf parsley, roughly chopped

EQUIPMENT

Mini food processor

Kettle

Large pot with lid

Chef pan

Cup and spoon measures

Large mixing bowl

2 chopping boards

Colander

2 knives

Tin opener

Spatula

Large slotted spoon

Tongs

Large shallow serving bowl

1 Put 2 litres of water in the large pot over a high heat. Add the cooking salt and put the lid on. Boil a kettleful of water and top up the pot. When the water is boiling rapidly, add the pasta. Put the lid back on for a minute or until the water comes back to a rapid boil.

2 Place the chef pan over a high heat. Cut the chicken into 3 pieces each. Place the flour in a large mixing bowl. Toss the chicken in the flour and shake off any excess.

3 Pour the oil into the pan and swirl to coat. Place the floured chicken skin-side down in the pan and leave it for about 5 minutes until golden brown.

4 Peel the garlic and peel and quarter the onion. Place in a mini food processor and blitz until finely chopped. Turn the chicken over and push it to one side of the pan. In the empty side of the pan, sauté the onion, garlic, tomato paste and oregano leaves for 2 minutes until soft and fragrant. Add the tomatoes, salt, pepper and wine and simmer for around 5 minutes. Distribute the chicken evenly through the sauce and bring back to the boil. Cook, stirring with a spatula, for 5 minutes. Add the olives and simmer for another 5 minutes with the lid off.

5 While the chicken is simmering, drain the pasta and put in the serving bowl. Roughly chop the parsley. Pour the chicken and sauce over the pasta and scatter with parsley. Serve to the table in the pan.

CHORIZO AND SPINACH PASTA

INGREDIENTS

1 tablespoon cooking salt

375 g dried small spiral pasta

2 chorizo sausages

1 red onion

½ jar (130 g) chargrilled capsicum,
   cut into strips

2 garlic cloves

¼ bunch basil

40 g block of parmesan

50 g baby spinach

Salt and ground black pepper

EQUIPMENT

Kettle

Large pot with lid

Chef pan

Spoon measures

2 chopping boards

2 knives

Fine grater

Large slotted spoon

Wooden spoon

Tongs

Garlic crusher

1 Put 2 litres of water in the large pot over a high heat. Add the cooking salt and put the lid on. Boil a kettleful of water and top up the pot. When the water is boiling rapidly, add the pasta. Put the lid back on for a minute or until the water comes back to a rapid boil.

2 Place the chef pan over a high heat. Slice the chorizo ½ cm thick on one board and place in the pan. Peel the onion and roughly dice on the second board. Place about a tablespoon of the oil from the capsicum jar in the pan. Lower the heat and add the onion. Crush the garlic directly into the pan. Cook, stirring occasionally.

3 Pick the basil leaves ready to mix through the pasta.

4 When the pasta is cooked, lift it out with a slotted spoon and place into the chef pan with the chorizo mixture. Grate the parmesan into the pan, add the spinach, basil and capsicum, and stir through. Taste and season with salt and pepper. (Chorizo and parmesan can both be salty so you may not need any salt.) Serve to the table in the pan.

NOTE › BUY THE CHORIZO FROM THE DELI, NOT THE KIND YOU BUY IN THE SAUSAGE SECTION OF THE BUTCHER'S.

GARLIC PRAWN SPAGHETTI

INGREDIENTS

1 tablespoon cooking salt

375 g dried thin spaghetti

2 teaspoons olive oil

300 g raw prawn meat

40 g butter

4 garlic cloves

½ cup white wine (or chicken stock)

1 cup thickened cream

2 tablespoons Dijon mustard

½ teaspoon ground white pepper

2 teaspoons cornflour

Salt to taste

1 tablespoon olive oil

1 teaspoon red wine vinegar

100 g mixed salad leaves

Ground black pepper to serve

EQUIPMENT

Kettle

Large pot with lid

Chef pan

Cup and spoon measures

2 mixing bowls, large and small

2 chopping boards

2 knives

Wooden spoon

Tongs

Garlic crusher

Pasta server

Fork

Serving platter

1 Put 2 litres of water in the large pot over a high heat. Add the cooking salt and put the lid on. Boil a kettleful of water and top up the pot. When the water is boiling rapidly, add the spaghetti. Put the lid back on for a minute or until the water comes back to a rapid boil.

2 Put the chef pan over a medium heat. Add the olive oil and sauté the prawns until just cooked. Remove to the small bowl. Add the butter into the pan and crush the garlic into it. Stir for about 2 minutes, until soft and fragrant. Add the wine and cook for a further minute. Pour in the cream and add the mustard and pepper. Dissolve the cornflour in a little water and stir into the sauce. Cook for 3–4 minutes until the sauce has thickened. Taste and add salt.

3 While the sauce is cooking, place the olive oil and red wine vinegar in the large mixing bowl and whisk lightly with a fork. Toss through the salad leaves and place the dressed salad on a serving platter on the table.

4 Take ½ cup sauce out of the pan and place in the mixing bowl with the prawns. Put the spaghetti in the pan and mix thoroughly to coat. Divide the spaghetti between 4 bowls. Divide the prawns between the bowls and sprinkle with pepper.

NOTE › BUY AUSTRALIAN FROZEN RAW PRAWN MEAT IN SUPERMARKETS OR AT THE FISHMONGER.

CHICKEN AND LEMON TAGINE

INGREDIENTS

⅓ cup olive oil

800 g skinless chicken thigh fillets

4 garlic cloves

1 large onion

2 teaspoons sea salt

1 tablespoon ground turmeric

1 tablespoon ground cumin

1 lemon

1 cup chicken stock

1 cup water

1 cup pearl couscous

12 large green olives

¼ bunch flat-leaf parsley

EQUIPMENT

Food processor

Chef pan with lid

Cup and spoon measures

Large mixing bowl

2 chopping boards

2 knives

Fine grater

Citrus squeezer

Spoon

Tongs

1 Put the chef pan over a high heat with 2 tablespoons olive oil in it.

2 Cut the chicken thighs into 3 pieces each. Peel the garlic and peel and quarter the onion. Place the garlic, onion, salt, turmeric, cumin and 3 tablespoons oil into a food processor. Zest and juice the lemon into the processor and blitz until a smooth thick paste is achieved. Place in a large bowl and toss the chicken through.

3 Place the coated chicken in the hot oil. Leave it, not turning or stirring, for 3 minutes or until it is a lovely golden brown colour. Turn the chicken over and carefully pour the stock into the pan with the water. Bring to the boil then turn the heat down to low.

4 Using a spoon, nestle the pearl couscous around the sides of the chicken pieces, making sure that it is submerged in the liquid. Place the olives around the pan. Put the lid on the pan and simmer without stirring for 12–15 minutes or until the couscous is cooked and the liquid is almost all absorbed.

5 While the chicken is simmering, remove the stalks from the parsley and roughly chop the leaves. Scatter the parsley over the chicken and serve to the table in the pan.

MUSHROOM FETTUCCINE

INGREDIENTS

1 tablespoon cooking salt
500 g fresh fettuccine
800 g cup mushrooms
1 tablespoon olive oil
25 g butter
3 garlic cloves
¼ cup tomato paste
2 tablespoons plain flour
1 cup beef stock
½ cup thickened cream
Salt and ground black pepper
20 g block of parmesan

EQUIPMENT

Kettle
Large pot with lid
Chef pan
Cup and spoon measures
Chopping board
Colander
Knife
Fine grater
Wooden spoon
Garlic crusher

1 Put 2 litres of water in the large pot over a high heat. Add the cooking salt and put the lid on. Boil a kettleful of water and top up the pot. When the water is boiling rapidly, add the fettuccine. Put the lid back on for a minute or until the water comes back to a rapid boil.

2 Put the chef pan over a medium-high heat. Slice the mushrooms into about 4 pieces each.

3 Heat the oil and butter in the pan until the butter is frothing. Add the mushrooms and let them cook for about 6 minutes. They will release a lot of liquid, which will eventually evaporate. When the mushrooms start to turn golden, crush the garlic into the pan.

4 Add the tomato paste to the pan. Sprinkle the flour over the mixture and stir for a minute. Add the stock, ½ cup at a time, allowing the sauce to come to the boil after each addition. Add the cream and stir to combine. Taste and season with salt and pepper.

5 When the fettuccine is cooked, strain in the colander. Stir through the sauce and serve to the table in the pan. Put the block of parmesan and the fine grater on the table so everyone can grate their own.

CHICKEN AND CHORIZO STEW

INGREDIENTS

800 g tin chopped tomatoes

½ teaspoon salt

¼ teaspoon ground black pepper

½ cup risoni pasta

1 cup beef stock

1 tablespoon olive oil

2 chorizo sausages

500 g chicken thigh fillets

1 garlic clove

1 brown onion

1 long red chilli

½ green capsicum

½ cup tomato paste

2 small zucchini

EQUIPMENT

Food processor

Large pot

Chef pan

Cup and spoon measures

2 chopping boards

2 knives

Tin opener

Wooden spoon

Teaspoon

1 Place the pot over a high heat. Add the tomatoes, salt, pepper, risoni and beef stock. Bring to the boil, stirring occasionally.

2 Put the chef pan with the olive oil in it over a high heat. Cut the chorizo into 1 cm slices. Cut the chicken thighs into 3 pieces each. Put them in the chef pan and brown on one side.

3 Peel the garlic and peel and quarter the onion. Cut the chilli in half lengthways and scrape out the seeds with a teaspoon. Cut off the stalk and discard along with the seeds. Cut the 4 sides and the base off the capsicum. Put the onion, garlic, chilli and capsicum in the food processor and blitz until very finely diced.

4 Place this mixture in the pan with the chicken and chorizo and stir together for 2 minutes, until the capsicum mixture is softened and fragrant. Add the tomato paste and stir. Tip the contents of the pot into the chef pan and stir together. Cut the zucchini into 1 cm thick slices and add to the pan. Sauté for another 3 minutes or until the risoni is cooked and the zucchini tender. Serve to the table in the pan.

NOTE › BUY THE CHORIZO FROM THE DELI, NOT THE KIND YOU BUY IN THE SAUSAGE SECTION OF THE BUTCHER'S.

MINESTRONE

INGREDIENTS

1 litre beef stock

800 g tin crushed tomatoes

1 large potato

1 cup risoni pasta

4 rashers bacon

1 tablespoon olive oil

2 carrots

2 celery stalks

2 brown onions

400 g tin red kidney beans

Salt and pepper

40 g block of parmesan

4 slices sourdough bread, for serving

EQUIPMENT

Large pot with lid

Chef pan

Cup and spoon measures

2 chopping boards

Colander

2 knives

Tin opener

Wooden spoon

Vegetable peeler

Ladle

1   Place the large pot over a high heat. Pour in the beef stock and tomatoes and bring to the boil. While the stock is coming to the boil, peel the potato and slice 1 cm thick. Cut the slices into cubes and add to the pot with the stock. Once the pot comes back to the boil, add the risoni.

2   Put the chef pan over a medium-high heat. Strip the rind off the bacon and cut crossways into 1 cm strips. Add to the chef pan along with the olive oil. Stir occasionally until the bacon starts to go golden brown.

3   While the bacon is cooking, peel the carrots and cut in half lengthways. Slice into 1 cm pieces and put in the pan. Slice the celery 1 cm thick and put into the pan. Peel and roughly chop the onions and add to the pan. Sauté for about 5 minutes, until softened and fragrant.

4   While the vegetables are sautéing and the risoni and potato are cooking, empty the kidney beans into a colander and rinse. Add to the pot with the stock and tomatoes. Tip the contents of the chef pan into the pot. Simmer until the risoni and potato are both cooked. Taste and season with salt and pepper.

5   Ladle into bowls and use a vegetable peeler to shave some parmesan on top of each bowl. Serve with bread.

NOTE › IF THERE IS ANY SOUP LEFT OVER, THE RISONI WILL ABSORB ALL THE STOCK. JUST ADD A LITTLE MORE STOCK WHEN REHEATING TO LOOSEN IT BACK UP.

HEARTY CHICKEN SOUP

INGREDIENTS

4 chicken thigh fillets

1 tablespoon olive oil

2 medium carrots

2 brown onions

3 celery stalks

¼ cup plain flour

2 litres chicken stock

1 cup risoni pasta

Salt and pepper

EQUIPMENT

Large pot

Cup and spoon measures

2 chopping boards

2 knives

Wooden spoon

Vegetable peeler

Ladle

1 Heat the pot over a medium-high heat. Cut the chicken thighs into about 8 pieces each. Place the oil in the pot and add the chicken. Stir once or twice to make sure the chicken does not stick.

2 While the chicken cooks, peel the carrots. Cut their tops off and halve them lengthways. Cut into 1 cm pieces. Place in the pot with the chicken and stir. Cut the tops off the onions, cut in half and peel. Cut into a fairly large dice, about the same size as the carrots. Put in the pot and stir. Cut the celery stalks in half lengthways and cut into 1 cm pieces. Add to the pot.

3 Add the flour and stir to coat the contents of the pot. Add the stock, ½ cup at a time, until all the flour is incorporated, then add the rest of the stock. Bring to the boil and add the risoni. Boil rapidly for another 6–8 minutes or until the risoni is al dente. Taste and season with salt and pepper. Ladle into bowls and serve.

NOTE > IF THERE IS ANY SOUP LEFT OVER, THE RISONI WILL ABSORB ALL THE STOCK. JUST ADD A LITTLE MORE STOCK WHEN REHEATING TO LOOSEN IT BACK UP.

CHILLI TUNA SPAGHETTI WITH MIXED LEAVES

INGREDIENTS

1 tablespoon cooking salt

375 g dried thin spaghetti

2 garlic cloves

2 brown onions

1 long red chilli

2 tablespoons olive oil

800 g tin crushed tomatoes

½ teaspoon dried oregano leaves

1 teaspoon salt

½ teaspoon black pepper

2 teaspoons sugar

2 tablespoons red wine vinegar

100 g mixed salad leaves

425 g tin tuna in brine

½ cup cream

EQUIPMENT

Mini food processor

Kettle

Large pot with lid

Chef pan

Measuring jug

Cup and spoon measures

Chopping board

Knife

Tin opener

Wooden spoon

Teaspoon

Tongs

Serving bowl

1 Put 2 litres of water in the large pot over a high heat. Add the cooking salt and put the lid on. Boil a kettleful of water and top up the pot. When the water is boiling rapidly, add the spaghetti. Put the lid back on for a minute or until the water comes back to a rapid boil.

2 Put the chef pan over a medium heat.

3 Peel the garlic and peel and quarter the onions. Cut the chilli in half lengthways and scrape the seeds out with a teaspoon. Discard the seeds and stalk. Place the garlic, onion and chilli in the mini food processor and blitz until finely chopped.

4 Place half the olive oil in the chef pan and add the onion mixture. Sauté, stirring, for about 2 minutes or until soft and fragrant. Add the tomatoes, oregano, salt, pepper, sugar and a tablespoon of the red wine vinegar. Raise the heat to high and simmer rapidly, stirring occasionally, until the sauce thickens and becomes richly fragrant. This will take 5–6 minutes.

5 While the sauce simmers, place the salad leaves in a serving bowl and open and drain the tuna. Add the tuna and the cream to the pan and turn the heat off. When the spaghetti is al dente, remove from the boiling water with tongs and place in the pan with the sauce. Gently stir the spaghetti through the sauce. Don't be too vigorous at this stage, the tuna should break into chunks but not become mushy.

6 Drizzle the remaining red wine and olive oil over the salad leaves and toss lightly. Serve to the table, alongside the spaghetti in the pan.

CHEESY MAC WITH PEAS AND CORN

INGREDIENTS

1 tablespoon cooking salt

375 g dried macaroni or small spirals

50 g butter

⅓ cup plain flour

3½ cups milk

1 tablespoon Dijon mustard

2 cups grated tasty cheese

400 g tin sweet corn kernels

1 cup frozen baby peas

½ teaspoon salt

¼ teaspoon ground white pepper

EQUIPMENT

Kettle

Large pot with lid

Chef pan

Cup and spoon measures

Colander

Wooden spoon

1 Put 2 litres of water in the large pot over a high heat. Add the cooking salt and put the lid on. Boil a kettleful of water and top up the pot. When the water is boiling rapidly, add the macaroni. Put the lid back on for a minute or until the water comes back to a rapid boil.

2 Place the chef pan over a medium-high heat. Melt the butter and add the flour. Stir constantly with a wooden spoon until it is mixed and starts to froth a little. Continue to stir for another minute or so. This begins to cook the flour.

3 Add a little milk – about ¼ cup – and stir. This will incorporate fairly quickly. It will come away from the sides of the pan and look like dough. Once this happens you can add another ¼ cup milk and repeat until all the milk has been added. Stir in the mustard, then add the cheese and stir until it melts.

4 When the macaroni is cooked, strain it through the colander. Tip it into the chef pan and stir it through the cheese sauce. Add the corn and peas and stir until the peas are fully defrosted and everything is warmed through. Taste and season with salt and pepper.

VARY IT – STILL UNDER $20: ADD A COUPLE OF HANDFULS OF ONE OR TWO OF THE FOLLOWING: CHOPPED COOKED BACON, SLICED SHALLOTS, FRESH HERBS, CHOPPED SEMI-DRIED TOMATOES, TINNED TUNA, SLICED COOKED MUSHROOMS, OR ANY NUMBER OF OTHER INGREDIENTS. GREAT FOR USING UP LEFTOVERS, TOO.

BY THE TIME THE PASTA IS COOKED,
THE REST OF THE MEAL WILL BE TOO!

20|20

PESTO PASTA

INGREDIENTS

1 tablespoon cooking salt

375 g dried thin spaghetti

100 g pine nuts

¼ teaspoon salt

¼ teaspoon ground black pepper

½ cup extra virgin olive oil

½ bunch basil

2 garlic cloves

50 g block of parmesan

1 punnet grape tomatoes

1 lemon

25 g feta

EQUIPMENT

Food processor

Kettle

Large pot with lid

Medium frypan

Spoon measures

Chopping board

Colander

Knife

Fine grater

Citrus squeezer

Spatula

Wooden spoon

Tongs

Serving platter

1 Put 2 litres of water in the large pot over a high heat. Add the cooking salt and put the lid on. Boil a kettleful of water and top up the pot. When the water is boiling rapidly, add the spaghetti. Put the lid back on for a minute or until the water comes back to a rapid boil.

2 Place the frypan over a medium-high heat and add the pine nuts. Once the pan is hot the pine nuts will quickly go golden. Remove them from the pan, reserving a couple of tablespoons for serving. Place in the food processor, along with the salt, pepper and all but a dash of the olive oil. Pick the leaves off the basil and place in the food processor. Peel the garlic and pop it in. Roughly chop the parmesan into chunks and place in the food processor. Blitz until the pesto is well combined, but still a little chunky.

3 Put a dash of olive oil in the frypan and toss the tomatoes until they blister slightly.

4 When the spaghetti is cooked, strain into a colander. Tip back into the pot and add the pesto. Zest the lemon into the pot and squeeze the juice over. Slide onto a serving platter, crumble the feta over the top and scatter with the tomatoes and pine nuts.

HONEY MUSTARD CHICKEN WITH BROCCOLINI PASTA

INGREDIENTS

1 tablespoon cooking salt

Half of a 375 g packet of dried small spiral pasta

2 large chicken breast fillets (250 g each)

1 tablespoon olive oil

1 bunch broccolini (240 g)

20 g butter

40 g block of parmesan

½ cup white wine

¼ cup wholegrain mustard

¼ cup honey

⅓ cup cream

Salt and ground white pepper, to taste

EQUIPMENT

Kettle

Large pot with lid

Chef pan

Cup and spoon measures

Large mixing bowl

2 chopping boards

Colander

2 knives

Fine grater

Spatula

Large slotted spoon

Wooden spoon

Tongs

Meat mallet

Foil

Plate

1 Put the chef pan over a medium-high heat. Put 2 litres of water in the large pot over a high heat. Add the cooking salt and put the lid on. Boil a kettleful of water and top up the pot. When the water is boiling rapidly, add the spirals. Put the lid back on for a minute or until the water comes back to a rapid boil.

2 Cut the chicken breast in half horizontally and hammer gently with a meat mallet to flatten it so that it is a uniform thickness (about 5 mm). Put the oil in the pan and cook the chicken for about 3 minutes on each side, until golden brown and just cooked through. Remove to a plate and cover with foil. Turn the heat off.

3 While the chicken is cooking, trim the ends off the broccolini and cut diagonally into 3 cm lengths. Add to the pot with the pasta. Once cooked (about 2 minutes), remove from the water with a slotted spoon and place in the large mixing bowl with the butter. Once the pasta is cooked, strain it through a colander and tip into the bowl with the broccolini. Grate the parmesan over and stir through. Taste and season if necessary.

4 While the pasta cooks, turn the heat back on the chef pan. Pour the wine into the pan and use a spatula to collect any nice brown bits from the bottom. Add the mustard, honey and half of the cream and bring to the boil, stirring. Cook for a couple of minutes. Stir in the rest of the cream and remove from the heat. Taste and season with salt and pepper.

5 Divide the chicken between 4 plates. Top with the pasta and pour the sauce over the top.

SMOKED SALMON SPAGHETTI

INGREDIENTS

1 tablespoon cooking salt

375 g dried thin spaghetti

2 slices bread (stale, if available)

1 tablespoon olive oil

2 tablespoons baby capers

2 garlic cloves

125 g cream cheese

¼ cup cream

1 lemon

1 tablespoon Dijon mustard

100 g smoked salmon

¼ bunch dill

50 g baby spinach

1 teaspoon salt

½ teaspoon ground white pepper

EQUIPMENT

Mini food processor

Kettle

Large pot with lid

Chef pan

Cup and spoon measures

Large mixing bowl

2 chopping boards

2 knives

Fine grater

Citrus squeezer

Wooden spoon

Tongs

Garlic crusher

Ladle

Paper towel

1 Put the chef pan over a medium heat. Put 2 litres of water in the large pot over a high heat. Add the cooking salt and put the lid on. Boil a kettleful of water and top up the pot. When the water is boiling rapidly, add the spaghetti. Put the lid back on for a minute or until the water comes back to a rapid boil.

2 Tear the bread into chunks and put into the mini food processor. Blitz until you have a mixture of fine crumbs and fingernail-sized chunks. Pour the oil into the pan and add the bread. Stir for a couple of minutes until it starts to go golden brown. Add the baby capers and crush the garlic into the pan. Stir everything together and cook until the crumbs are golden and crisp. Tip the mixture out of the pan into the bowl and wipe the pan out with paper towel.

3 Lower the heat and roughly chop the cream cheese into the pan. Add the cream. Zest about half the lemon into the pan. Cut the lemon in half and squeeze the juice of one half into the pan. Add the Dijon mustard. Stir everything together and allow to gently melt.

4 Cut the smoked salmon into strips. Tear the fronds off the dill.

5 When the spaghetti is cooked, lift it out of the pot with tongs and transfer directly to the pan. The water from the spaghetti will help the sauce to loosen and melt. Add the dill, smoked salmon, spinach, salt and pepper and stir gently through. If the sauce needs to loosen up a bit, ladle in a little of the pasta water. Serve in bowls topped with the crispy breadcrumbs and capers.

VIETNAMESE-STYLE NOODLE SOUP

INGREDIENTS

2 litres chicken stock

2 cm piece of ginger

2 garlic cloves

1 long green chilli

4 shallots

½ bunch coriander

400 g fresh rice noodles

1 bunch choy sum

1 small red chilli

2 tablespoons fish sauce

1 cup bean sprouts

¼ bunch mint leaves

EQUIPMENT

Kettle

2 large pots

Medium mixing bowl

Chopping board

Colander

Wire mesh strainer

Knife

4 noodle bowls

1 Put the chicken stock into one of the pots over a high heat and bring to the boil. Cut the unpeeled ginger in half and add to the pot. Cut the unpeeled garlic cloves in half and add to the pot. Halve the green chilli lengthways and add to the pot. Cut the shallots into long pieces and add them to the pot. Cut the stems and roots off the coriander, reserving the leaves. Wash the stems and roots under the tap and add to the pot. Boil rapidly.

2 Boil the kettle. Place the noodles in the mixing bowl and pour the boiling water over them. Strain through a colander and divide between 4 bowls.

3 Cut the choy sum into 1 cm pieces and divide between the 4 bowls, placing on top of the noodles. Slice the red chilli and set aside.

4 Pour the chicken stock through the wire strainer into the clean pot. Discard the contents of the strainer. Bring the stock back to the boil. Add the fish sauce.

5 Pour the stock into the 4 bowls. Top each bowl with ¼ of the bean sprouts, some coriander and mint leaves, and the sliced chilli.

PASTA BOSCAIOLA

INGREDIENTS

1 tablespoon cooking salt

375 g dried small pasta spirals

2 tablespoons olive oil

250 g cup or button mushrooms

2 garlic cloves

200 g sliced ham

1 tablespoon cornflour

½ cup white wine

1 cup thickened cream

Salt and ground white pepper

4 shallots

20 g block of parmesan

EQUIPMENT

Kettle

Large pot with lid

Chef pan

Cup and spoon measures

2 chopping boards

Colander

2 knives

Fine grater

Wooden spoon

Garlic crusher

1 Put 2 litres of water in the large pot over a high heat. Add the cooking salt and put the lid on. Boil a kettleful of water and top up the pot. When the water is boiling rapidly, add the pasta. Put the lid back on for a minute or until the water comes back to a rapid boil.

2 Put the chef pan over a medium-high heat with the oil in it. Slice the mushrooms thickly into 3 or 4 pieces each and add to the pan. Give them a stir and cook for about 3 minutes or until starting to turn golden. Crush the garlic into the pan.

3 Roll the ham up and slice into strips. Add to the pan. Sprinkle the cornflour over the mixture and stir for a minute. Add the wine and bring to the boil. Add the cream and stir to combine. Bring to the boil and let it bubble for a couple of minutes until the pasta is ready. Taste and season with salt and pepper.

4 While the pasta cooks, peel and slice the shallots. When the pasta is cooked, strain it through the colander. Stir the pasta and shallots through the sauce and serve at the table in the pan with the block of parmesan and the fine grater.

NOTE › BUY LEG HAM OFF THE BONE IF YOUR DELI SELLS IT.

PAPPARDELLE WITH SPECK, PEAS AND SHALLOTS

INGREDIENTS

1 tablespoon cooking salt

375 g packet fresh lasagne sheets

150 g piece of speck

4 shallots

¾ cup frozen baby peas

½ cup thickened cream

½ teaspoon sea salt flakes

¼ teaspoon ground white pepper

40 g block of parmesan

EQUIPMENT

Kettle

Large pot with lid

Chef pan

2 chopping boards

Colander

2 knives

Fine grater

Tongs

1 Put 2 litres of water in the large pot over a high heat. Add the cooking salt and put the lid on. Boil a kettleful of water and top up the pot.

2 Take the lasagne sheets out of the packet and, without unrolling them, cut into 2 cm wide strips. When the water is boiling rapidly, separate the ribbons of pasta and drop them into the pot. Put the lid back on for a minute or until the water comes back to a rapid boil. The pasta will only need to cook for a few minutes, as it is fresh not dried. Strain in the colander.

3 While the pasta cooks, put the chef pan over a medium-high heat. Peel the rind off the piece of speck and cut it into slices, then into batons. Put it in the pan and cook until the fat melts and the speck is starting to turn golden. While it cooks, slice up the shallots. Add the peas, shallots, and cream to the pan. Add the drained pasta to the pan and toss to coat. Taste and season with salt and pepper. Serve in bowls and grate parmesan over.

NOTE › SPECK CAN BE FOUND AT MOST DELI COUNTERS. IF IT IS NOT AVAILABLE, USE BACON INSTEAD.

TUNA MORNAY

INGREDIENTS

1 tablespoon cooking salt
200 g dried macaroni
2 small carrots
1 brown onion
50 g butter
½ of a 400 g tin sweet corn kernels
½ cup frozen baby peas
¼ cup plain flour
2 cups milk
2 tablespoons Dijon mustard
1 cup grated tasty cheese
425 g tin tuna in brine
¼ teaspoon salt
¼ teaspoon ground white pepper

EQUIPMENT

Mini food processor
Kettle
Large pot with lid
Chef pan
Large measuring jug
Measuring spoons
Chopping board
Colander
Knife
Tin opener
Wooden spoon
Tongs
Vegetable peeler

1 Put 2 litres of water in the large pot over a high heat. Add the cooking salt and place the lid on. Boil a kettleful of water and top up the pot. When the water is boiling rapidly, add the macaroni. Stir and put the lid back on for a minute or until the water comes back to a rapid boil.

2 Place the chef pan over medium heat. Peel the carrots. Quarter lengthways and cut into 1 cm pieces. Peel and quarter the onion and blitz in the mini food processor until finely diced. Melt the butter in the pan and add the carrot, onion, corn kernels and peas. Stir for 3–4 minutes until the carrots are starting to soften. Sprinkle the flour over the pan and stir to coat the vegetables well.

3 Pour in ½ cup milk and stir until it is all incorporated and starting to form a thick,

doughy sauce. Add another ½ cup and repeat. Add the last of the milk and cook for a minute more, stirring.

4 Add the mustard and cheese and stir until the cheese has melted. Drain the tuna and add to the pan. Break up any huge lumps but don't stir too much after this or the tuna will disintegrate and become mushy. Taste and season with salt and pepper.

5 When the macaroni is al dente, strain it through a colander and tip into the tuna sauce. Serve straight away.

NOTE: THIS DISH CAN BE REHEATED BUT THE PASTA WILL ABSORB MOST OF THE MOISTURE WHEN IT IS STORED. JUST ADD A LITTLE MILK TO LOOSEN IT BACK UP WHEN REHEATING.

SWEET AND SOUR VEGGIE NOODLES

INGREDIENTS

400 g packet Hokkien noodles

1 red onion

2 zucchini

1 carrot

1 red capsicum

2 teaspoons peanut or vegetable oil

440 g tin pineapple pieces in juice

¼ cup white vinegar

1 tablespoon cornflour

½ cup tomato sauce

1 tablespoon light soy sauce

4 shallots

½ bunch coriander

¼ cup crispy fried shallots

EQUIPMENT

Kettle

Chef pan

Large measuring jug

Cup and spoon measures

Large mixing bowl

Chopping board

Colander

Mandolin/V-slicer with plain and julienne
    attachments

Knife

Tin opener

Wooden spoon

Tongs

Fork

Serving platter

1 Place the noodles in the mixing bowl. Boil a
   kettleful of water and pour over the noodles.
   After about 1 minute, drain in the colander.

2 Peel the onion and slice with the plain blade
   of the mandolin. Replace with the julienne
   attachment and use to julienne the zucchini.
   Place in a mixing bowl. Peel the carrot and do
   the same. Cut the 4 sides off the capsicum and
   slice into strips. Add all the vegetables to the
   mixing bowl and toss to combine.

3 Put the chef pan over a medium-high heat with
   the oil in it. Place the vegetables in the pan
   and sauté for 1–2 minutes. Drain the pineapple
   pieces, reserving the juice. Add the pineapple
   and noodles to the pan and turn down the heat.

4 Combine the reserved pineapple juice, vinegar,
   cornflour, tomato sauce and soy sauce in the
   measuring jug and mix thoroughly with a fork.
   Pour into the pan and stir until thickened and
   the cornflour has cooked, about 2–3 minutes.

5 While the sauce cooks, peel and slice the
   shallots and pick the leaves from the coriander.
   Remove the pan from the heat and slide the
   veggies and noodles onto a serving platter. Top
   with shallots, coriander leaves and crispy fried
   shallots.

PORK PAD THAI

INGREDIENTS

2 × 200 g packets shelf-fresh pad Thai noodles

1 cup roasted, unsalted peanuts

2 tablespoons peanut or vegetable oil

300 g pork fillet

4 shallots

½ bunch coriander

1 lime

¼ cup tamarind concentrate

¼ cup fish sauce

⅓ cup brown sugar

4 cloves garlic

2 eggs

1 cup bean sprouts

EQUIPMENT

Kettle

Chef pan

Cup and spoon measures

2 mixing bowls, large and small

Large measuring jug

2 chopping boards

Colander

2 knives

Wooden spoon

Tongs

Garlic crusher

Fork

Plate

Serving platter (optional)

1 Place the chef pan over a high heat. Boil the kettle. Put the noodles in the large bowl and pour the boiling water over them. Strain through the colander.

2 Place the peanuts in the pan and let them darken, even char slightly in some places. This will take a minute or so in an already hot pan. Remove the peanuts and add a tablespoon of oil to the pan.

3 Slice the pork into ½ cm thick pieces and place in the pan. Leave to cook for about a minute or until golden brown. Turn and cook on the other side for a further minute. Turn the heat off and remove the pork to the small bowl to prevent it from overcooking.

4 Roughly chop the roasted peanuts. Peel the shallots and cut into ½ cm pieces. Pick the leaves from the coriander. Cut the lime into 8 wedges. Place these garnishes aside on a plate ready for serving.

5 In the jug, combine the tamarind concentrate, fish sauce and brown sugar. Turn the heat under the pan back on and add the remaining oil. Crush the garlic, one clove at a time, into the pan. Stir through the noodles. Add the sauce and stir.

6 Push the noodle mixture to one side and crack the eggs into the pan. Break the yolks and gently stir the noodles again. Add the pork back in and heat through. Before serving, top with the shallots, coriander, peanuts and bean sprouts. Place the lime wedges around the side of the pan or serving platter.

SPAGHETTI NAPOLITANA WITH ITALIAN SALAD

INGREDIENTS

1 tablespoon cooking salt

375 g dried spaghetti

3 garlic cloves

2 brown onions

2 tablespoons olive oil

800 g tin crushed tomatoes

1 teaspoon dried oregano leaves

1 teaspoon salt

½ teaspoon black pepper

2 teaspoons sugar

100 g mixed salad leaves

1 ripe red tomato

½ small red onion

½ bunch basil

8 mini bocconcini

1 tablespoon balsamic glaze

½ teaspoon sea salt flakes

EQUIPMENT

Mini food processor

Kettle

Large pot with lid

Chef pan

Large measuring jug

Measuring spoons

Chopping board

Knife

Tin opener

Wooden spoon

Tongs

Salad bowl

1 Put 2 litres of water in the large pot over a high heat. Add the cooking salt and place the lid on. Boil a kettleful of water and top up the pot. When the water is boiling rapidly, add the spaghetti. Put the lid back on for a minute or until the water comes back to a rapid boil.

2 Put the chef pan over a medium heat.

3 Peel the garlic and peel and quarter the onions. Place them in the mini food processor and blitz until finely chopped.

4 Place a tablespoon of olive oil in the chef pan and add the onion mixture. Sauté, stirring, for about 2 minutes or until soft and fragrant. Add the tinned tomatoes, oregano, salt, pepper and sugar. Raise the heat to high and simmer rapidly, stirring occasionally until the sauce thickens and becomes richly fragrant. This will take 5–6 minutes.

5 While the sauce simmers, place the salad leaves in a serving bowl. Cut the tomato into wedges. Peel and thinly slice the red onion. Pick half the basil leaves. Add all these to the lettuce in the bowl along with the bocconcini. Drizzle with remaining olive oil, the balsamic glaze and the sea salt, and toss lightly.

6 When the spaghetti is al dente, remove from the boiling water with tongs and place in the pan with the sauce. Gently stir the spaghetti through the sauce. Pick the remaining basil leaves and stir through. Serve to the table in the pan alongside the salad.

CHICKEN NOODLES WITH OYSTER SAUCE

INGREDIENTS

2 teaspoons peanut or vegetable oil

2 chicken thigh fillets

400 g packet Hokkien noodles

1 red capsicum

1 red onion

1 bunch pak choy

⅓ cup oyster sauce

2 tablespoons light soy sauce

½ bunch coriander

Crispy fried garlic

EQUIPMENT

Kettle

Chef pan

Cup and spoon measures

Mixing bowl

Large measuring jug

2 chopping boards

Colander

2 knives

Wooden spoon

Serving platter

1 Put the chef pan over a medium-high heat with the oil in it. Cut the chicken thighs into strips and place in the pan.

2 Place the noodles in the mixing bowl. Boil a kettleful of water and pour over the noodles. After about 1 minute, drain in the colander.

3 Cut the 4 sides off the capsicum and slice into strips. Peel the onion, halve and slice. Roughly chop the pak choy.

4 Place the vegetables in the pan and sauté for 1–2 minutes. Add the noodles to the pan and turn down the heat.

5 Add the oyster and soy sauces to the pan. When the chicken is cooked through, remove from the heat. Pick the coriander leaves and scatter on top along with the crispy fried garlic. Serve to the table in the pan.

NOTE › CRISPY FRIED GARLIC IS AVAILABLE IN THE ASIAN SECTION OF LARGE SUPERMARKETS OR AT THE ASIAN GROCER. IF YOU CAN'T FIND IT, USE CRISPY FRIED SHALLOTS INSTEAD.

RACE THE
RICE

♪♪BASMATI-RICE♪♪

CE♥♥

I HAVE COOKED MY RICE THE SAME WAY FOR YEARS –
IN A MICROWAVE RICE COOKER, WHICH IS REALLY
JUST A LARGE MICROWAVE-SAFE CONTAINER WITH A
TIGHT-FITTING LID. COOKED THIS WAY, IT TAKES
18 MINUTES, AND I HAVE ALWAYS MADE A BIT OF A
GAME OUT OF HAVING THE REST OF THE MEAL READY
BY THE TIME THOSE 18 MINUTES ARE UP.
READY, SET, RACE!

RECIPES

BACON AND TOMATO CHEAT'S RISOTTO

INGREDIENTS

1½ cups arborio rice

1 litre chicken stock

4 rashers bacon

135 g (half a jar) semi-dried tomatoes

1 garlic clove

1 brown onion

½ cup white wine (or stock)

½ bunch basil

20 g butter

50 g block of parmesan

Salt and pepper

EQUIPMENT

Mini food processor

Chef pan

Microwave rice cooker

Cup and spoon measures

2 chopping boards

2 knives

Fine grater

Wooden spoon

1   Put the rice in the rice cooker with 3 cups of stock and put the lid on. Microwave on high for 18 minutes.

2   Put the chef pan over a medium-high heat. Strip the rind off the bacon and cut into 1 cm thick strips. While the bacon cooks, cut the semi-dried tomatoes into rough chunks. Add to the pan with the bacon and lower the heat.

3   Peel the garlic and peel and quarter the onion. Place in the mini food processor and blitz until finely chopped. Add to the pan and stir for 2 minutes until soft and fragrant. Add the wine to the pan and stir. Add the rest of the chicken stock and bring to the boil. Pick the basil leaves off the stalks and set aside.

4   When the rice in the microwave has finished cooking, stir it into the pan. Add the butter and grate in the parmesan and stir again. Taste and season with salt and pepper, and stir through the basil leaves.

CHICKEN STROGANOFF

INGREDIENTS

2 cups long-grain rice (jasmine or basmati
    are fine)

⅓ cup plain flour

½ teaspoon salt

¼ teaspoon ground white pepper

2 teaspoons smoked sweet paprika (plus an
    extra pinch, to serve)

800 g chicken thigh fillets

1 tablespoon olive oil

12 small or 6 medium cup mushrooms

1 bunch broccolini

3 garlic cloves

¼ cup tomato paste

½ cup chicken stock

2 tablespoons Worcestershire sauce

300 ml sour cream

EQUIPMENT

Chef pan with lid

Microwave rice cooker

Cup and spoon measures

Large mixing bowl

2 chopping boards

2 knives

Wooden spoon

Tongs

Garlic crusher

Fork

1 Put the chef pan over a high heat. Put the rice in the rice cooker with 3 cups of water and put the lid on. Microwave on high for 18 minutes.

2 In a large bowl, combine the flour, salt, pepper and paprika. Cut the chicken thighs into strips, about 6 per thigh, and toss through the seasoned flour. Put the oil in the chef pan and place the chicken in the pan.

3 Halve the mushrooms (or quarter them if they are larger). Cut the broccolini diagonally into 3 cm long pieces.

4 Turn the chicken over and push it to one side of the pan. Add the mushrooms in the cleared space. Crush the garlic directly into the pan with the mushrooms. Add the tomato paste and stir the whole pan together, and allow to cook for one minute. Add the stock, Worcestershire sauce, broccolini and stir. Put the lid on and simmer for 3 minutes, or until the chicken is cooked and the broccolini tender. Add the sour cream and stir for a minute until hot through. Sprinkle a pinch of paprika over the top.

5 Remove the rice from the microwave and fluff with a fork. Serve alongside the stroganoff.

CHILLI CON CARNE

INGREDIENTS

2 tablespoons olive oil

2 cups long-grain rice (jasmine or basmati
  are fine)

500 g beef mince

2 cloves garlic

2 medium onions

3 long green chillies

1½ teaspoons ground cumin

1½ teaspoons smoked paprika

2 tablespoons tomato paste

400 g tin red kidney beans

800 g tin chopped tomatoes

1 cup beef stock

Salt and ground black pepper

1 teaspoon chilli powder

300 ml sour cream

EQUIPMENT

Food processor

Chef pan

Microwave rice cooker

Cup and spoon measures

Chopping board

Colander

Knife

Tin opener

Wooden spoon

Fork

1 Put the chef pan over a high heat with the oil in it. Put the rice in the rice cooker with 3 cups of water and put the lid on. Microwave on high for 18 minutes.

2 Place the beef mince in the pan, breaking up any lumps with a wooden spoon. Cook until browned.

3 While the beef cooks, peel the garlic and peel and halve the onions. Halve the chillies lengthways, scrape out the seeds and discard the seeds and stalks. Put the garlic, onion, fresh chilli, cumin, paprika and tomato paste in the food processor and blitz to a puree.

4 Add the puree to the pan and stir for 3 minutes. Tip the kidney beans into the colander and rinse under the tap. Add the beans to the pan along with the tomatoes and stock. Bring to the boil and simmer rapidly until the rice is ready. If the mixture dries out too much, add a little water and turn the heat down. Taste and season with salt and pepper.

5 Remove the rice from the microwave and fluff with a fork. Serve at the table with the chilli powder and sour cream on the side for people to help themselves.

CURRIED EGGS

INGREDIENTS

2 cups basmati rice

8 eggs (55 g each, room temperature)

1 brown onion

1 tablespoon olive oil

1 tablespoon tomato paste

1 tablespoon curry powder

1 tablespoon brown sugar

2 tablespoons plain flour

2½ cups milk

1 cup frozen baby peas

Salt and pepper

¼ bunch flat-leaf parsley

EQUIPMENT

Chef pan

Medium pot

Microwave rice cooker

Cup and spoon measures

Medium mixing bowl

Chopping board

Knife

Large slotted spoon

Wooden spoon

Kitchen scissors

Fork

1 Put the rice in the rice cooker with 3 cups of water and put the lid on. Microwave on high for 18 minutes.

2 Half fill a medium pot with water and put over a high heat until the water is at a rapid boil. Half fill the mixing bowl with cold water from the tap. Lower the eggs into the boiling water and cook for 6 minutes. Using a large slotted spoon, remove the eggs from the boiling water and place in the bowl of cold water.

3 While the eggs cook, heat the chef pan over a medium heat. Peel and halve the onion, then slice it. Put the olive oil in the pan and sauté the onions until soft and fragrant. Add the tomato paste and sauté for a further minute. Add the curry powder and sugar and stir for another minute. Add the flour and mix well – it will form a doughy mixture. Add the milk, ½ cup at a time, and cook well between additions. Add the baby peas.

4 Shell the eggs and cut into quarters. Add to the pot and heat through. Taste and season with salt and pepper. Snip the leaves of the parsley over the dish. Remove the rice from the microwave and fluff with a fork. Serve to the table with the curried eggs.

MEXICAN BEEF AND BEANS

INGREDIENTS

1 tablespoon olive oil

2 cups long-grain rice (jasmine or basmati
 are fine)

300 g beef mince

2 garlic cloves

1 brown onion

2 teaspoons ground cumin seed

2 teaspoons smoked paprika

¼ teaspoon ground chilli

¼ cup tomato paste

2 tablespoons plain flour

400 g tin crushed tomatoes

1 teaspoon salt

400 g tin red kidney beans

1 avocado

1 lemon

Salt and ground white pepper

½ cup sour cream

½ cup grated tasty cheese

EQUIPMENT

Mini food processor

Chef pan

Microwave rice cooker

Small mixing bowl

Chopping board

Colander

Knife

Tin opener

Citrus squeezer

Spoon

Wooden spoon

2 forks

1 Put the chef pan over a high heat with the oil in it. Put the rice in the rice cooker with 3 cups of water and put the lid on. Microwave on high for 18 minutes.

2 Place the beef mince in the pan and stir, using the spoon to break up any lumps.

3 Peel the garlic and peel and quarter the onion. Place in the mini food processor. Blitz until finely chopped. Add to the mince in the pan. Stir for about 2 minutes, until fragrant. Add the cumin, paprika, chilli and tomato paste, and stir for another minute.

4 Sprinkle the flour over the pan and stir through. Add the tinned tomatoes and salt.

Cook for about 5 minutes until thick and rich. Drain the beans in the colander and rinse under running water. Stir the beans through the mixture.

5 While the beef is cooking, cut the avocado in half and scoop out the flesh with a spoon. Place in the small mixing bowl and squeeze half of the lemon into it. Mash roughly with a fork and season with salt and pepper to taste.

6 Remove the rice from the microwave and fluff with a fork. Divide into 4 bowls and top with the beef mixture, a dollop of avocado and sour cream, and a scattering of grated tasty cheese.

QUICK FRIED RICE

INGREDIENTS

1 tablespoon peanut oil

2 cups jasmine rice

3 eggs

4 rashers bacon

1 chicken thigh fillet

2 garlic cloves

1 medium brown onion

1 cup frozen baby peas

400 g tin sweet corn kernels

1 teaspoon Chinese five-spice

¼ cup light soy sauce

¼ bunch coriander

½ cup crispy fried shallots

EQUIPMENT

Mini food processor

Chef pan

Microwave rice cooker

Cup and spoon measures

Small mixing bowl

2 chopping boards

2 knives

Tin opener

Spatula

Wooden spoon

Whisk

Fork

1 Put the chef pan over a medium-high heat with the oil in it. Put the rice in the rice cooker with 3 cups of water and put the lid on. Microwave on high for 18 minutes.

2 Lightly whisk the eggs in the mixing bowl with about a tablespoon of water. Tip into the pan and swirl to coat the bottom. After about 30 seconds the egg should be starting to set. Use the spatula to roll the egg up from one side of the pan to the other and lift out onto the chopping board.

3 Strip the rind off the bacon and cut into 1 cm strips. Cook for 1–2 minutes, stirring occasionally. Cut the chicken thigh fillet into small pieces, about 1 cm cubes. Put in the pan with the bacon and stir.

4 While the chicken and bacon are cooking, peel the garlic and peel and quarter the onion. Place in the mini food processor. Blitz until finely chopped and add to the pan. Cook for 1–2 minutes.

5 While the onion and garlic are cooking, roughly chop the egg into strips and add to the pan. Add the frozen peas. Drain the corn and add to the pan.

6 When the rice is cooked, fluff with a fork and tip into the pan. Sprinkle the five-spice and soy sauce over the top and stir with the spatula for a minute until well combined.

7 Pick the leaves off the coriander and scatter them over the rice along with the crispy fried shallots.

CHILLI PLUM CHICKEN

INGREDIENTS

2 cups jasmine rice

800 g chicken thigh fillets

2 tablespoons peanut oil

2 garlic cloves

½ cup plum jam

¼ cup soy sauce

2 tablespoons hot chilli sauce

¼ cup rice wine vinegar

1 teaspoon ground ginger

1 teaspoon cornflour

20 snow peas

6 shallots

2 tablespoons sesame seeds

EQUIPMENT

Chef pan with lid

Wok (or second frypan)

Microwave rice cooker

Large measuring jug

Cup and spoon measures

Small mixing bowl

2 chopping boards

2 knives

Spatula

2 pairs of tongs

Garlic crusher

Whisk

Fork

Serving platter

1 Put the chef pan over a high heat. Put the rice in the rice cooker with 3 cups of water and put the lid on. Microwave on high for 18 minutes.

2 Cut the chicken thighs into 3 pieces each. Put a tablespoon of oil into the pan and add the chicken. Leave the chicken for 3 minutes to brown. Crush the garlic into the measuring jug, add the plum jam, soy sauce, hot chilli sauce, vinegar, ginger and cornflour, and whisk to combine. Turn the chicken over in the pan, and pour the plum sauce all over it.

3 Take the string out of the snow peas by grasping the stalk and peeling along the edge. Remove the outer layer of the shallots and cut them into 3 cm lengths.

4 Put the wok over a medium-high heat. Toast the sesame seeds until light golden brown. This will only take moments. Remove from the wok to the bowl with the spatula. Crank the heat up and add the rest of the oil. Add the snow peas and shallots and toss with tongs until lightly coated. Add 2 tablespoons of water. Cook for about 2 minutes, tossing occasionally, until the vegetables have softened a little but still retain their vibrant green colour. Remove from the heat.

5 Give the chicken a bit of a stir. It should be cooked through and the sauce reduced to a lovely thick consistency. Stir the vegetables through the chicken and then tip onto a serving platter. Scatter the sesame seeds over the top. Remove the rice from the microwave and fluff with a fork. Serve alongside the chicken.

EGGPLANT, ZUCCHINI AND CHICKPEA CURRY

INGREDIENTS

2 cups basmati rice

2 tablespoons vegetable oil

2 garlic cloves

1 red onion

¼ cup Thai red curry paste

1 medium eggplant

2 zucchini

400 g tin crushed tomatoes

400 ml tin coconut cream

400 g tin chickpeas

1 tablespoon brown sugar

1 tablespoon fish sauce

¼ bunch coriander

EQUIPMENT

Mini food processor

Chef pan

Microwave rice cooker

Cup and spoon measures

Chopping board

Colander

Knife

Tin opener

Wooden spoon

Vegetable peeler

Fork

1 Put the rice in the rice cooker with 3 cups of water and put the lid on. Microwave on high for 18 minutes.

2 Put the chef pan over a medium heat with the oil in it. Peel the garlic and peel and quarter the onion. Place them in the mini food processor and blitz until finely chopped. Put the onion and garlic mixture in the pan and cook gently for 1–2 minutes. Stir occasionally. Add the curry paste and continue to cook for a minute.

3 Peel the eggplant and slice 2 cm thick. Cut the slices into cubes and add to the pan. Cut the zucchini in quarters lengthways and then into 2 cm pieces. Add to the pan and mix everything together.

4 Add the tomatoes and coconut cream to the pan. Stir and bring to the boil. Strain the chickpeas in the colander and rinse under the tap. Add to the pan and bring back to the boil. Simmer rapidly until the eggplant has cooked through – about 6 minutes. Remove from the heat and add the brown sugar and fish sauce. (Taste to see if it needs more of either of those things.) Scatter with the coriander leaves. Remove the rice from the microwave and fluff with a fork. Serve to the table with the curry.

PEA AND LEMON CHEAT'S RISOTTO

INGREDIENTS

1½ cups arborio rice

1 litre chicken stock

1 tablespoon olive oil

1 garlic clove

1 brown onion

1 lemon

½ cup white wine (or stock)

1 cup frozen baby peas

20 g butter

50 g block of parmesan

Salt and pepper

¼ bunch basil

EQUIPMENT

Mini food processor

Chef pan

Microwave rice cooker

Cup and spoon measures

Chopping board

Knife

Fine grater

Citrus squeezer

Wooden spoon

1 Put the rice in the rice cooker with 3 cups of stock and put the lid on. Microwave on high for 18 minutes.

2 Put the chef pan over a medium heat with the oil in it. Peel the garlic and peel and quarter the onion. Place in the mini food processor and blitz until finely chopped. Add to the pan and stir for 2 minutes until soft and fragrant. Zest the lemon into the pan. Add the wine to the pan and stir. Add the rest of the chicken stock and juice the lemon into the pan. Bring to the boil and add the peas.

3 Remove the rice from the microwave and stir it into the pan. Add the butter and grate in the parmesan and stir again. Taste and season with salt and pepper. Pick the leaves from the basil and stir through the risotto.

CHILLI CHICKEN STIR-FRY

INGREDIENTS

2 cups jasmine rice

800 g chicken thigh fillets

1 tablespoon + 1 teaspoon peanut or vegetable oil

4 cm piece of ginger

2 garlic cloves

1 long red chilli

½ cup sweet chilli sauce

¼ cup soy sauce

¼ cup white vinegar

1 teaspoon cornflour

1 bunch baby bok choy

6 shallots

EQUIPMENT

Chef pan

Wok

Microwave rice cooker

Large measuring jug

Cup and spoon measures

2 chopping boards

2 knives

Wooden spoon

Vegetable peeler

Garlic crusher

Grater

Fork

1 Put the chef pan over a high heat. Put the rice in the rice cooker with 3 cups of water and put the lid on. Microwave on high for 18 minutes.

2 Cut the chicken thighs into strips, about 8 pieces per thigh. Put a tablespoon of oil into the pan and add the chicken.

3 Peel and grate the ginger, crush the garlic and slice the chilli. Add them to the pan and stir through the chicken. Add the sweet chilli and soy sauce. Combine the vinegar and cornflour in the measuring jug and stir to dissolve. Pour into the pan with the chicken and stir through. Bring to the boil and allow to simmer for 6–7 minutes, stirring occasionally.

4 While the chicken simmers, cut the bok choy into quarters lengthways. Peel the shallots and cut into 3 cm lengths. Heat a teaspoon of oil in the wok over a high heat and stir-fry the bok choy and shallots with a splash of water for a minute or until just wilted. Remove from the heat.

5 Remove the rice from the microwave and fluff with a fork. Stir the greens through the chicken and serve to the table in the pan alongside the rice.

LAMB BIRYANI

INGREDIENTS

1½ cups basmati rice

2¾ cups beef stock

½ cup slivered almonds

2 tablespoons olive oil

500 g lamb mince

2 garlic cloves

2 brown onions

1 tablespoon curry powder

¼ teaspoon cinnamon

1 medium zucchini

400 g tin chopped tomatoes

1 lemon

¼ cup coriander leaves

½ cup plain Greek yoghurt

EQUIPMENT

Food processor

Chef pan

Microwave rice cooker

Cup and spoon measures

Chopping board

Knife

Tin opener

Wooden spoon

1 Put the rice and beef stock in the rice cooker and put the lid on. Microwave on high for 16 minutes.

2 Heat the chef pan over a medium-high heat and add the almonds. Toast until light golden brown and remove from the pan.

3 Add a tablespoon of oil to the hot pan. Sauté the lamb mince until starting to brown, stirring with a wooden spoon and squashing any lumps. Turn the heat down to medium-low.

4 While the lamb is cooking, peel the garlic and peel and quarter the onions. Place in the food processor. Blitz until finely chopped. Add the onions, garlic, curry powder and cinnamon to the pan and stir through the lamb. Cook for 1–2 minutes until soft and fragrant.

5 Cut the very bottom off the zucchini and quarter it lengthways. Cut into 1 cm thick pieces.

6 Add the tomatoes and zucchini to the lamb mixture. Turn the heat up to high and bring to the boil. Put the lid on the pan and cook for about 5 minutes. When the rice is cooked, remove from the microwave. Stir it through the lamb mixture and cook until the mixture is quite dry. Cut the lemon into 8 wedges. Serve the biryani at the table scattered with the almonds and coriander leaves, and yoghurt and lemon wedges on the side.

I HAVE ALWAYS MADE A BIT OF A GAME OUT
OF HAVING THE REST OF THE MEAL READY
BY THE TIME THE RICE IS COOKED.
READY, SET, RACE!

20|20

SESAME HOISIN CHICKEN

INGREDIENTS

2 cups jasmine rice

1 kg chicken thigh fillets

2 tablespoons peanut oil

½ cup hoisin sauce

¼ cup white vinegar

2 tablespoons soy sauce

2 bunches pak choy

3 fat shallots

2 tablespoons sesame seeds

¼ cup water

EQUIPMENT

Chef pan with lid

Wok (or second frypan)

Microwave rice cooker

Large measuring jug

Cup and spoon measures

Small mixing bowl

2 chopping boards

2 knives

Spatula

2 pairs of tongs

Fork

Serving platter

1 Put the chef pan over a medium-high heat. Put the rice in the rice cooker with 3 cups of water and put the lid on. Microwave on high for 18 minutes.

2 Cut the chicken thighs into 3 pieces each. Put a tablespoon of oil into the pan and add the chicken. Leave the chicken for 3 minutes to brown. Combine the hoisin sauce, vinegar and soy sauce in the measuring jug. Turn the chicken over and pour the sauce all over it. Put the lid on the pan.

3 Wash the pak choy to remove any grit. Cut into quarters lengthways. Remove the outer layer of the shallots and cut into 3 cm lengths.

4 Put the wok over a medium-high heat. Toast the sesame seeds until light golden brown. This will only take moments. Remove from the wok to the bowl with a spatula. Crank the heat up and add the rest of the oil. Add the pak choy and toss with tongs until lightly coated. Add the shallots and ¼ cup water. Remove the lid from the chicken and put it over the wok. Cook for about 5 minutes, tossing occasionally, until the pak choy has softened but still retains its vibrant green colour. Remove it from the heat.

5 Give the chicken a bit of a stir. It should be cooked through and the sauce reduced to a lovely thick consistency. Place the vegetables on a platter and tip the chicken over the top, using a spatula to make sure none of the delicious sauce is wasted. Scatter with sesame seeds. Remove the rice from the microwave and fluff with a fork. Serve alongside the chicken platter.

THAI-STYLE RED FISH CURRY

INGREDIENTS

2 cups jasmine rice

400 g white fish fillets

12 green beans

1 small zucchini

1 teaspoon peanut oil

¼ cup red curry paste

400 ml tin coconut cream

225 g tin pineapple chunks

225 g tin bamboo shoots

1 tablespoon brown sugar

1 tablespoon fish sauce

2 tablespoons lime juice

EQUIPMENT

Wok

Microwave rice cooker

Cup and spoon measures

2 chopping boards

2 knives

Tin opener

Citrus squeezer

Wooden spoon

Vegetable peeler

Fork

1 Put the rice in the rice cooker with 3 cups of water and put the lid on. Microwave on high for 18 minutes.

2 Cut the fish fillets into 3 cm pieces. Trim the tops off the beans (the end that was attached to the plant) and cut them in half. Use the vegetable peeler to cut the zucchini into ribbons.

3 Put the wok over a medium-high heat. Add the peanut oil and curry paste and stir for a minute, until fragrant. Add the coconut cream and bring to a simmer.

4 Open and drain the pineapple and bamboo shoots and add to the wok. Bring back to a simmer.

5 Gently lower the fish into the coconut cream along with the beans. After a couple of minutes, add the zucchini ribbons, brown sugar and fish sauce. Bring back to a simmer and then remove from the heat. Add the lime juice. Taste and add a little more fish sauce or sugar if it needs more saltiness or sweetness.

6 Remove the rice from the rice cooker and fluff with a fork. Serve with the curry.

EASY CHICKEN CURRY WITH CUCUMBER SALAD

INGREDIENTS

2 cups basmati rice

1 kg chicken thigh fillets

1 tablespoon peanut or vegetable oil

2 garlic cloves

1 large brown onion

2 tablespoons curry powder

2 tablespoons tomato paste

¼ cup brown sugar

1¾ cups natural yoghurt

½ cup frozen baby peas

2 Lebanese cucumbers

¼ bunch mint

1 lemon

Salt and ground black pepper

EQUIPMENT

Mini food processor

Chef pan

Microwave rice cooker

Cup and spoon measures

Medium mixing bowl

2 chopping boards

Wire mesh strainer

2 knives

Wooden spoon

Teaspoon

Tongs

Fork

1   Put the chef pan over a high heat. Put the rice in the rice cooker with 3 cups of water and put the lid on. Microwave on high for 18 minutes.

2   Cut the chicken thighs into 3 pieces each. Put the oil into the pan and add the chicken. Leave the chicken for 3 minutes to brown.

3   Peel the garlic and peel and quarter the onion. Place them in the mini food processor. Blitz until finely chopped.

4   Turn the chicken pieces over and push them to one side of the pan. Put the onion mixture and the curry powder in the empty side of the pan and sauté, stirring for 1–2 minutes until starting to soften. Add the tomato paste and sugar to the pan and stir the chicken through the mixture. Add a cup of the yoghurt and bring to a simmer, stirring. Simmer uncovered for about 5 minutes or until the chicken is cooked through.

5   While the chicken is simmering, place the frozen peas in the mixing bowl with some water to defrost. Halve the cucumbers lengthways and use a teaspoon to scrape out the seeds. Slice diagonally. Strain the peas and put them back in the bowl along with the cucumber. Tear the mint leaves into the bowl and add ¼ cup yoghurt, lemon juice and a pinch of salt and pepper. Toss with tongs to combine.

6   Stir the last ½ cup of yoghurt through the curry and remove the pan from the heat. Season to taste, and add a little more sugar if needed.

7   Remove the rice from the microwave, fluff with a fork and serve alongside the curry and cucumber salad.

NASI GORENG

INGREDIENTS

1 tablespoon peanut oil

2 cups jasmine rice

2 chicken thigh fillets

2 garlic cloves

1 brown onion

2 teaspoons shrimp paste

½ cup light soy sauce

½ cup brown sugar

1 Lebanese cucumber

1 ripe tomato

3 shallots

1 long red chilli

4 eggs

2 tablespoons hot chilli sauce

¼ cup crispy fried shallots

¼ cup roasted salted peanuts

EQUIPMENT

Mini food processor

Chef pan

Medium frypan

Microwave rice cooker

Cup and spoon measures

Bowl

2 chopping boards

2 knives

Wooden spoon

Egg flip

1   Put the chef pan over a high heat with half the oil in it. Put the rice in the rice cooker with 3 cups of water and put the lid on. Microwave on high for 18 minutes.

2   Cut the chicken thighs into strips, about 8 pieces each. Place the chicken in the pan.

3   Peel the garlic and peel and quarter the onion. Place in the mini food processor and blitz until finely chopped. Add to the chicken in the pan and stir for a minute or until starting to soften. Add the shrimp paste and stir through, cooking for a further minute. When the chicken is cooked through, turn off the heat.

4   In a bowl, combine the soy sauce and the brown sugar. Slice the Lebanese cucumber finely on the diagonal. Slice the tomato. Peel the shallots and slice. Slice the long red chilli.

5   Heat the frypan over a medium-high heat and add the remaining oil. Fry the eggs sunny side up.

6   Turn the chef pan back on and pour in half the soy sauce mixture and the chilli sauce. When the rice is cooked, tip it into the pan and stir to mix thoroughly.

7   Divide the rice among 4 plates and top with equal amounts of crispy shallots, shallots, chilli and peanuts. Place one egg on the top of each plate and put the cucumber and tomato beside the rice. Serve with the remaining sweetened soy sauce.

NOTE › SHRIMP PASTE AND CRISPY FRIED SHALLOTS CAN BE FOUND IN THE ASIAN SECTION OF LARGE SUPERMARKETS, OR IN ASIAN GROCERY STORES.

OLD-FASHIONED CURRIED SAUSAGES

INGREDIENTS

2 cups basmati rice

800 g good-quality thin beef sausages

2 large brown onions

2 tablespoons olive oil

2 tablespoons curry powder

2 tablespoons flour

400 ml tin apricot nectar

400 g tin crushed tomatoes

2 teaspoons salt

½ cup green mango chutney

1 cup frozen baby peas

EQUIPMENT

Chef pan

Medium frypan

Microwave rice cooker

Cup and spoon measures

2 chopping boards

2 knives

Tin opener

Wooden spoon

Tongs

1 Put the rice in the rice cooker with 3 cups of water and put the lid on. Microwave on high for 18 minutes.

2 Place the frypan over a medium-high heat. Place the sausages in the pan and cook for 6–7 minutes, turning occasionally, until browned all over.

3 While the sausages are cooking, put the chef pan over a medium-high heat. Peel and halve the onions and slice them thickly. Put the olive oil in the pan and sauté the onions for 2 minutes, or until softening. Add the curry powder and cook for another minute.

4 When the sausages are browned all over, turn the heat off the frypan. Let them rest while you prepare the sauce.

5 Add the flour to the onion and stir. Pour in a little of the apricot nectar and stir until thickened. Continue to add the rest of the nectar bit by bit, stirring as you go. Add the tomatoes, salt and chutney.

6 Cut the sausages on the diagonal into 2 cm lengths and put them in the chef pan with the sauce. Simmer, stirring, until the sauce has thickened and the sausages are cooked through. Add the baby peas in the last 2 minutes of cooking and heat through. Remove the rice from the microwave, fluff with a fork and serve alongside the curried sausages.

NOTE › GREEN MANGO CHUTNEY CAN BE FOUND WITH THE INDIAN INGREDIENTS IN THE SUPERMARKET.

SESAME-CRUSTED FISH WITH ASIAN GREENS

INGREDIENTS

2 cups jasmine rice

1 bunch choy sum

½ bunch shallots

2 tablespoons peanut or vegetable oil

¼ cup sesame seeds

4 × 120 g boneless, skinless white fish fillets

3 cm piece of ginger

2 garlic cloves

2 cups fish or chicken stock

2 tablespoons soy sauce

EQUIPMENT

Chef pan

Microwave rice cooker

Cup and spoon measures

Shallow dish

Chopping board

Knife

Tongs

Egg flip

Garlic crusher

Ladle

Fork

Plate

1 Put the rice in the rice cooker with 3 cups of water and put the lid on. Microwave on high for 18 minutes.

2 Cut the choy sum into 5 cm lengths. Peel the shallots and cut into 5 cm lengths. Set aside.

3 Heat the chef pan over a medium-high heat and add a tablespoon of oil.

4 Place the sesame seeds in a shallow dish. Dip the fish portions, one side only, into the sesame seeds. Place the fish, seed side down, in the pan and cook for 2–3 minutes or until the sesame seeds are golden and the fish is turning opaque. Flip carefully and cook for a further minute or two. The cooking time will depend on the thickness of the fish. Once cooked, remove the fish from the pan and put on the clean plate, seed side up, to rest.

5 Peel the ginger. Reduce the heat to medium and add the remaining oil. Grate the ginger and crush the garlic into the pan and sauté for a minute or until soft and fragrant. Raise the heat and toss through the choy sum and shallots. Pour in a little fish or chicken stock, then add the soy sauce. Pour in the rest of the stock and bring back to the boil. Remove from the heat and ladle the broth and vegetables into 4 bowls. Top each bowl with a piece of fish. Remove the rice from the microwave and fluff with a fork. Serve alongside the fish.

CURRIED CHICKEN RICE

INGREDIENTS

2 cups basmati rice

3 cups chicken stock

2 chicken thigh fillets

2 tablespoons olive oil

¼ bunch coriander

2 garlic cloves

2 brown onions

440 g tin crushed pineapple in juice

½ cup currants

1 tablespoon curry powder

½ teaspoon salt

1 tablespoon white wine vinegar

½ cup roasted salted peanuts

EQUIPMENT

Food processor

Chef pan

Microwave rice cooker

Cup and spoon measures

2 chopping boards

2 knives

Tin opener

Spatula

Wooden spoon

1 Put the chef pan over a high heat. Put the rice in the rice cooker with 3 cups of chicken stock and put the lid on. Microwave on high for 18 minutes.

2 Cut the chicken thighs into small pieces, about a 2 cm dice. Put the oil in the pan and add the chicken. Cook for 3–4 minutes, stirring occasionally.

3 While the chicken cooks, pull the leaves off the coriander and reserve. Wash the stems and roots thoroughly and put them in the food processor. Peel the garlic and peel and quarter the onions. Put them in the food processor too. Blitz until finely chopped. You will need to scrape down the sides of the food processor once or twice. Tip the contents into the pan with the chicken. Cook for 1–2 minutes.

4 Add the undrained contents of the pineapple tin to the pan and add the currants, curry powder, salt and vinegar. Bring to the boil. Mash the currants with the wooden spoon as you cook them, to break them up a bit.

5 When the rice has cooked, tip it into the pan and stir through. Serve to the table in the pan topped with peanuts and coriander leaves.

THAI-STYLE GREEN PRAWN CURRY

INGREDIENTS

2 cups jasmine rice

1 small zucchini

1 teaspoon peanut oil

¼ cup green curry paste

400 ml tin coconut cream

225 g tin bamboo shoots

300 g raw prawn meat

1 tablespoon brown sugar

1 tablespoon fish sauce

1 lime

¼ bunch coriander

EQUIPMENT

Wok

Microwave rice cooker

Spoon measures

Chopping board

Knife

Tin opener

Citrus squeezer

Wooden spoon

Vegetable peeler

1 Put the rice in the rice cooker with 3 cups of water and put the lid on. Microwave on high for 18 minutes.

2 Use the vegetable peeler to cut the zucchini into ribbons.

3 Put the wok over a medium-high heat. Add the peanut oil and curry paste and stir for a minute, until fragrant. Add the coconut cream and bring to a simmer.

4 Open and drain the bamboo shoots and add to the wok. Bring back to a simmer.

5 Place the prawn meat into the simmering coconut cream. After a couple of minutes, add the zucchini ribbons, brown sugar and fish sauce. Bring back to a simmer and then remove from the heat. Juice the lime into the wok. Taste and add a little more fish sauce or sugar if it needs more saltiness or sweetness. Pick the leaves from the coriander and scatter over the curry.

6 Remove the rice from the rice cooker and fluff with a fork. Serve with the curry.

SWEET AND SOUR PORK MEATBALLS

INGREDIENTS

2 cups jasmine rice

500 g pork mince

1 teaspoon garlic powder

½ teaspoon chilli powder

¼ teaspoon salt

1 cup breadcrumbs

1 egg

1 tablespoon peanut oil

1 green capsicum

2 brown onions

440 g tin pineapple pieces in juice

¼ cup white vinegar

1 tablespoon cornflour

½ cup tomato sauce

1 tablespoon light soy sauce

EQUIPMENT

Chef pan

Microwave rice cooker

Large measuring jug

Cup and spoon measures

Large mixing bowl

Chopping board

Knife

Tin opener

Wooden spoon

Fork

1 Put the rice in the rice cooker with 3 cups of water and put the lid on. Microwave on high for 18 minutes.

2 Combine the pork mince, garlic powder, chilli powder, salt, breadcrumbs and egg in the large bowl. Using clean damp hands, very thoroughly combine the ingredients. Roll the mixture into golf ball–sized rounds, keeping your hands damp as you go. When you have just a few balls to go, put the chef pan over a medium-high heat and add the oil.

3 Fry the meatballs for about 5 minutes or until brown. Shake the pan back and forth occasionally to cook them on all sides.

4 While the meatballs cook, slice two sides off the capsicum and cut into 2 cm squares. Peel and halve the onions and cut into a large dice, about 2 cm.

5 Put the onion and capsicum in the pan with the meatballs and stir. Open and drain the pineapple, reserving the juice. Put the pineapple pieces in the pan.

6 Combine the reserved pineapple juice, vinegar, cornflour, tomato sauce and soy sauce in the measuring jug. Mix thoroughly with a fork. Pour into the pan and stir until thickened and the cornflour has cooked, about 2–3 minutes. Remove the rice from the microwave and fluff with a fork. Serve the meatballs to the table in the pan alongside the rice.

BEEF AND PEANUT STIR-FRY

INGREDIENTS

2 cups jasmine rice

500 g rump steak

2 tablespoons peanut or vegetable oil

12 green beans

6 shallots

2 garlic cloves

½ cup oyster sauce

2 tablespoons soy sauce

¼ cup roasted, salted peanuts

EQUIPMENT

Chef pan

Microwave rice cooker

Cup and spoon measures

2 chopping boards

2 knives

Wooden spoon

Tongs

Garlic crusher

Fork

1 Put the chef pan over a high heat. Put the rice in the rice cooker with 3 cups of water and put the lid on. Microwave on high for 18 minutes.

2 Trim any thick fat off the rump steak and slice the beef as thinly as you can. When the pan is very hot, add the oil and then the beef. Using tongs, spread the meat around so that each piece is in direct contact with the surface of the pan. Let it sizzle away undisturbed for a couple of minutes or until the cooked side of the meat is a lovely golden colour.

3 While the meat cooks, cut the stalk end off the beans and cut them in half. Peel the shallots and cut into 3 cm lengths. Add the beans and shallots to the pan. Crush the garlic into the pan and stir everything together. Stir in the oyster and soy sauces. Let the beans and shallots warm through and remove the pan from the heat.

4 Roughly chop the peanuts. Remove the rice from the microwave and fluff with a fork. Scatter the peanuts over the stir-fry and serve at the table with the rice.

ON A
ROLL

WITH SO MANY BEAUTIFUL TYPES OF BREAD
AVAILABLE, TO SUIT ALL KINDS OF DIETARY NEEDS
AND TASTES, MEALS ARE EASIER THAN EVER. BREAD
ALLOWS YOU TO ADD THE CARBOHYDRATE PORTION
OF THE MEAL WITH VERY LITTLE EFFORT – AND OF
COURSE IT'S DELICIOUS TOO. HOPEFULLY THE RECIPES
IN THIS CHAPTER ARE A SPRINGBOARD FOR MORE
IDEAS THAT YOUR FAMILY WILL LOVE. FRESH,
SIMPLE AND FAST – DINNER IS ON A ROLL!

RECIPES

CHICKEN BURRITOS 150

FISH BURGERS 153

THREE-CHEESE QUESADILLAS 154

GOURMET STEAK SANDWICH 157

LAMB KOFTA PIZZA 158

CHICKEN WALDORF SALAD
ON SOURDOUGH 161

STEAK BURRITOS 162

HAM, AVOCADO AND PINEAPPLE
PIZZA SUBS 165

CHICKEN CAESAR BURGERS

INGREDIENTS
1 loaf Turkish bread
4 rashers bacon
2 large chicken breast fillets
Salt and pepper
2 teaspoons olive oil
4 eggs
1 baby cos lettuce
1 small red onion
½ cup creamy caesar salad dressing
40 g block of parmesan
Barbecue sauce (optional)

EQUIPMENT
Oven
Medium frypan
Grill plate
Cup measures
3 chopping boards
2 knives
Bread knife
Tongs
Vegetable peeler
Egg flip
Meat mallet
Timer
Foil
Paper towel

1 Preheat the oven to 200°C. Put the grill plate over a high heat.

2 Put the Turkish bread in the oven and set a timer for 5 minutes while you get on with the rest of the meal. When the timer goes off, remove the bread from the oven.

3 Strip the rind off the bacon and cut into thirds. Place on the grill plate and cook until golden and starting to crisp – about 3–4 minutes. Cut the chicken breasts in half horizontally and hammer gently with a meat mallet to flatten them so that they are a uniform thickness (about 5 mm). Remove the bacon from the pan and set aside on paper towel.

4 Place the chicken on the grill plate and cook for about 3 minutes each side, or until lightly golden and cooked through. Remove from grill and set aside to rest. Season with salt and pepper and cover with foil.

5 Heat the frypan over a medium heat and add the olive oil. Fry the eggs to your liking. Remove and put on a plate.

6 While the eggs are frying, remove 6–8 leaves from the cos lettuce. Wipe off any dirt and then trim the hard white bits and any tired leathery bits from the tips. Cut into pieces. Peel and thinly slice the red onion into rounds.

7 Using the bread knife, slice the Turkish bread horizontally all the way along. Spread the caesar dressing along the bottom. Top with the cos lettuce and onion. Using the vegetable peeler, peel strips of parmesan on top of the lettuce. Top with the chicken, bacon and eggs. Season with pepper and squeeze on some barbecue sauce if you like. Cover with the top slice and, using the bread knife, carefully cut into quarters and serve.

ANTIPASTI PIZZA

INGREDIENTS

4 pizza bases (about 20 cm)

1 cup tomato pizza sauce

1 cup grated mozzarella cheese

1 cup grated tasty cheese

1 red onion

½ of a 260 g jar chargrilled capsicum

¼ cup sliced, pitted kalamata olives

50 g feta

1 Lebanese cucumber

2 shallots

1 tablespoon olive oil

1 teaspoon balsamic vinegar

100 g baby spinach

EQUIPMENT

Oven

2 large baking trays

Cup and spoon measures

Large mixing bowl

Chopping board

Knife

Spoon

Pizza cutter

Timer

Oven mitt

Fork

Baking paper

Serving platter

1 Preheat the oven to 200°C. Line the baking trays with baking paper and place 2 bases on each.

2 With the back of a spoon, spread pizza sauce on each base. Top with the grated mozzarella and tasty cheese.

3 Peel and roughly chop the onion. Divide the onion, capsicum and olives between the pizzas, then crumble a little feta over each one. Place in the oven for 4 minutes. (Set the timer.) Swap the top and bottom trays and cook for a further 4–6 minutes.

4 While the pizzas cook, cut the cucumber into quarters lengthways, then into 2 cm lengths. Peel and chop the shallots. Place the olive oil and balsamic vinegar in the large mixing bowl and whisk lightly with a fork. Toss through the spinach, cucumber and shallots and place on the serving platter on the table.

5 Slide the pizzas onto a board and serve to the table with the cutter.

NOTE › FOR THIS RECIPE I TRIED A FEW DIFFERENT PRE-MADE PIZZA BASES. I HAD THE BEST SUCCESS WITH THE ONES THAT WERE FRESH (FROM THE BREAD SECTION OR THE BAKER), NOT REFRIGERATED OR FROZEN. THE ONES I LIKED BEST WEREN'T THE CHEAPEST BUT STILL FIT INTO THE $20 BUDGET.

PORK AND FENNEL HEROES WITH APPLE SLAW

INGREDIENTS

1 tablespoon whole fennel seeds

500 g good-quality pork sausages

¼ bunch fresh dill

2 tablespoons vegetable oil

⅓ cup mayonnaise

1 tablespoon white vinegar

1 bulb baby fennel

1 Granny Smith apple

4 shallots

4 long rolls

EQUIPMENT

Chef pan

Cup and spoon measures

2 mixing bowls, large and medium

Chopping board

Mandolin/V-slicer with plain and julienne
   attachments

Knife

Spoon

Tongs

1 Put the chef pan over a medium heat. Dry-fry the fennel seeds until fragrant. Remove to the medium mixing bowl.

2 Squeeze the sausages out of their skins into the mixing bowl with the fennel seeds. Chop the dill leaves and add to the bowl. Combine using clean damp hands and divide the mixture into quarters. Roll into a long oval then press flat. Raise the heat on the chef pan to medium-high and add oil. Fry the patties for about 4–5 minutes each side or until golden brown and just cooked through.

3 While the patties are cooking, put the mayonnaise and vinegar in the large mixing bowl and stir together. Reserve 2 tablespoons for rolls. Cut the bottom off the fennel and, using a mandolin, slice the bulb part into the mixing bowl. Using the julienne attachment of the mandolin, slice the unpeeled apple into the bowl. Peel and finely slice the shallots and add to the bowl. Toss to mix.

4 Spread the rolls with reserved dressing, and serve the pork patties on the rolls with the slaw.

TANDOORI CHICKEN WRAPS

INGREDIENTS

6 chicken thigh fillets (about 600 g)

¾ cup tandoori paste

1½ cups plain Greek yoghurt

½ iceberg lettuce

3 shallots

⅓ cup thick mint sauce

½ bunch coriander

4 large soft round flatbread wraps

1 lemon

EQUIPMENT

Oven grill

Baking dish

Cup and spoon measures

2 mixing bowls, large and small

2 chopping boards

2 knives

Spoon

Tongs

4 long metal skewers

1 Preheat the oven grill to 220°C. Cut the chicken thighs into 3 pieces each. In the large mixing bowl, combine the tandoori paste and half the yoghurt. Toss the chicken through the sauce. Thread the chicken onto metal skewers, making sure not to overcrowd them. Place the skewers across a baking dish so that the chicken is suspended over it.

2 Put the tray on the top shelf of the oven under the grill. Cook for 4–5 minutes, until the coating is dark with some black spots. Turn and cook for another 4–5 minutes. Remove from the grill and loosely cover with foil.

3 While the chicken is cooking and resting, finely slice the lettuce. Peel the shallots and slice them. In the small mixing bowl, combine the remaining yoghurt and mint sauce. Pick the leaves from the coriander. Cut the lemon into 8 wedges.

4 To serve, remove the chicken from the skewers, place the bread, chicken, lettuce, shallots, yoghurt sauce, lemon wedges and coriander leaves on the table so everyone can build their own wrap.

CHEAT'S SPINACH AND FETA GOZLEME

INGREDIENTS

¼ cup pine nuts

1 garlic clove

1 brown onion

3 tablespoons olive oil

100 g baby spinach

150 g feta

8 soft white round wraps

2 lemons

½ cup plain Greek yoghurt

EQUIPMENT

Mini food processor

Chef pan

Cup and spoon measures

Large mixing bowl

Chopping board

Knife

Wooden spoon

Egg flip

Pastry brush

Pizza cutter

Paper towel

1   Heat the chef pan over a medium heat. Dry-fry the pine nuts for 2–3 minutes or until golden brown. Keep a close eye on them as they can burn easily. Remove from the pan.

2   Peel the garlic and peel and quarter the onion. Place in the mini food processor and blitz until finely chopped. Add a teaspoon of oil to the pan and sauté the onion and garlic until soft and translucent. Remove from the pan to the mixing bowl and wipe the pan out with a paper towel.

3   Add the pine nuts, onion and garlic, spinach and crumbled feta to the bowl and stir to combine.

4   Brush a little more oil over the base of the pan and bring to a high heat. Place a wrap in the pan and spread one-eighth of the spinach mixture over half of the bread. Cook for about 30 seconds and then flip the empty half of the bread over the filling. Press flat with the egg flip. The bread should be golden. Remove to a board. Cut lemons into wedges.

5   Repeat the process with the remaining wraps. Cut into wedges and serve immediately with lemon and yoghurt on the side.

CHICKEN KEBABS WITH HOMMOUS

INGREDIENTS

1 tablespoon olive oil + ½ cup olive oil

2 teaspoons chilli powder

2 teaspoons sumac

2 teaspoons garlic powder

2 teaspoons onion powder

2¼ teaspoons salt

600 g chicken thigh fillets

400 g tin chickpeas

2 tablespoons tahini

2 garlic cloves

1 lemon

¼ iceberg lettuce

2 tomatoes

1 red onion

4 large pieces Lebanese bread

Barbecue or hot chilli sauce (optional)

EQUIPMENT

Food processor

Chef pan

Cup and spoon measures

Small mixing bowl

Shallow dish

2 chopping boards

Colander

2 knives

Tin opener

Citrus squeezer

Spatula

Spoon

Tongs

Meat mallet

Foil

Serving bowl, board and platter

1 Put the chef pan over a medium-high heat with 1 tablespoon oil in it. Place the dry spices and 2 teaspoons salt in the mixing bowl and stir to combine. Tip into a shallow dish. Hammer the chicken briefly with the meat mallet to flatten to about 1 cm thick. Dip each piece into the spice mix to coat. Put in the pan and cook on one side for 4–5 minutes. Turn and cook on the other side for a further 4–5 minutes or until cooked through. (The time will vary depending on how thinly you bashed the chicken.)

2 While the chicken is cooking, make the hommous. Tip the chickpeas into the colander and rinse under the tap. Place in the food processor with the tahini, ½ cup olive oil,

¼ teaspoon salt and peeled garlic cloves. Cut the lemon in half and squeeze juice into the processor. Blitz until it is a smooth puree. If it needs to be thinner, add some water a little at a time. Remove to a serving bowl.

3 Once the chicken is cooked, remove it from the pan and place on a board under foil.

4 Roughly chop the iceberg lettuce. Halve the tomatoes, cut out the stalk end, and slice. Halve, peel and slice the onion. Put the lettuce, tomato and onion on a platter alongside the Lebanese bread, chicken and hommous.

BARBECUE BACON PIZZA
WITH MIXED LEAVES

ON

INGREDIENTS

4 pizza bases (about 20 cm)

6 rashers bacon

1 red onion

1 cup barbecue sauce

1 cup grated mozzarella cheese

1 cup grated tasty cheese

1 tablespoon olive oil

1 teaspoon red wine vinegar

100 g mixed salad leaves

EQUIPMENT

Oven

Mini food processor

Chef pan

2 baking trays

Cup and spoon measures

2 chopping boards

2 knives

Spoon

Tongs

Timer

Oven mitt

Pizza cutter

Fork

Baking paper

Paper towel

Serving platter

1 Preheat the oven to 200°C. Put the chef pan over a medium-high heat. Line the baking trays with baking paper and place 2 bases on each.

2 Strip the rind off the bacon and slice roughly into 1 cm strips. Put into the chef pan and stir every now and then. When starting to become golden, remove from the pan to a paper towel to drain. While the bacon is cooking, peel and quarter the onion and put into the mini food processor. Blitz until roughly chopped.

3 With the back of the spoon, spread the barbecue sauce over the 4 pizza bases. Top each with ¼ cup mozzarella and ¼ cup grated tasty cheese. Top with the onion and the cooked bacon and place in the oven for 4 minutes. (Set the timer.) Swap the top and bottom trays and cook for a further 4–6 minutes.

4 Combine the olive oil and red wine vinegar in the large mixing bowl and whisk lightly with a fork. Toss through the salad leaves and place on a serving platter on the table.

5 Serve the pizzas at the table on a board with the pizza cutter and let everyone help themselves.

NOTE › FOR THIS RECIPE I TRIED A FEW DIFFERENT PRE-MADE PIZZA BASES. I HAD THE BEST SUCCESS WITH THE ONES THAT WERE FRESH (FROM THE BREAD SECTION OF THE SUPERMARKET OR THE BAKER) NOT REFRIGERATED OR FROZEN. THE ONES I LIKED BEST WEREN'T THE CHEAPEST BUT STILL FIT INTO THE $20 BUDGET.

CORN AND CAPSICUM QUESADILLAS

INGREDIENTS

400 g tin sweet corn kernels

1 green capsicum

1 red onion

1½ cups grated tasty cheese

¼ cup olive oil

8 soft white round wraps

1 avocado

½ cup tomato salsa

½ cup sour cream

EQUIPMENT

Food processor

Grill plate

Large mixing bowl

2 chopping boards

Knife

Tin opener

3 spoons

Wooden spoon

Tongs

Egg flip

Pastry brush

Pizza cutter

1 Heat the grill plate over a medium-high heat.

2 Drain the corn and place in the large mixing bowl. Cut the 4 sides and the base off the capsicum, and then peel and quarter the onion. Blitz in the food processor until finely chopped. Add to the corn in the mixing bowl and stir through the cheese.

3 Brush some oil on the grill plate. Place 2 wraps on the grill and top each with ¼ of the corn mixture. Spread to about 2 cm from the edge. Top each wrap with a second one and brush with oil. This should take 1–2 minutes. Using an egg flip (and tongs if necessary), carefully turn the whole round upside down and cook for a further minute. Remove to a chopping board and cut into 6 pieces with the pizza cutter.

4 Repeat with the next 4 wraps and filling. Divide the quesadillas between 4 plates.

5 Halve the avocado and run a knife through the flesh to create slices within the skin. Scoop out with a spoon and divide between the plates. Top with a dollop of salsa and sour cream, and serve.

LEBANESE LAMB BURGERS

INGREDIENTS

2 red onions

2 tablespoons olive oil

800 g lamb mince

1 tablespoon ground cumin

1 tablespoon garlic powder

1 teaspoon salt

¼ teaspoon ground black pepper

1 egg

1 cup breadcrumbs

2 ripe tomatoes

1 Lebanese cucumber

50 g rocket

½ cup plain Greek yoghurt

¼ cup thick mint sauce

4 soft white rolls or damper rolls

EQUIPMENT

Chef pan

Cup and spoon measures

2 mixing bowls, large and small

Chopping board

Knife

Spoon

Egg flip

1 Put the chef pan over a medium-high heat. Peel and halve the onions. Slice thickly and place in the pan with a tablespoon of oil. Stir occasionally.

2 While the onion cooks, put the lamb in the large mixing bowl with the cumin, garlic powder, salt, pepper, egg and breadcrumbs. Using clean damp hands, mix thoroughly until well combined and sticky. Divide the mixture into four and shape into round patties, 2 cm thick.

3 Remove the onion from the pan and add another tablespoon of olive oil. Place the patties in the pan and cook for about 5 minutes on each side, or until golden brown and just cooked through.

4 While the burgers cook, slice the tomato and cucumber. In the small mixing bowl, combine the yoghurt and mint sauce. To assemble the burgers, split the rolls in half horizontally. Place the lamb patty on the base and top with onion, rocket, tomato and cucumber. Dollop some mint yoghurt on top and cover with the other half of the roll.

BREAD ALLOWS YOU TO ADD THE CARBOHYDRATE
PORTION OF THE MEAL WITH VERY LITTLE EFFORT ...
FRESH, SIMPLE AND FAST!

20|20

CHICKEN BURRITOS

INGREDIENTS

800 g chicken thigh fillets
¼ cup plain flour
1½ tablespoons ground cumin
½ teaspoon salt
½ teaspoon ground white pepper
2 tablespoons olive oil
2 cloves garlic
1 large brown onion
3 long green chillies
¼ cup tomato paste
¼ cup white vinegar
¼ cup brown sugar
¼ cup water
½ iceberg lettuce
2 tomatoes
1 small red onion
8 soft flour burritos or wraps
½ cup sour cream (optional)
½ cup grated tasty cheese

EQUIPMENT

Mini food processor
Chef pan
Cup and spoon measures
Large mixing bowl
2 chopping boards
2 knives
Wooden spoon
Teaspoon
Tongs
Serving platter

1　Put the chef pan over a medium-high heat. Cut the chicken thighs into 3 pieces each and set aside.

2　Combine the flour, ground cumin, salt and pepper in the bowl. Toss the chicken in the mixture to coat. Shake off the excess flour. Place a tablespoon of oil in the pan and put the chicken in to brown on one side.

3　Peel the garlic and peel and quarter the onion. Halve the chillies lengthways and scrape out the seeds, discarding them along with the stalks. Blitz the garlic, onion and chillies in the mini food processor until finely chopped.

4　Turn the chicken over in the pan and push to one side. Pour the remaining oil in the empty part of the pan and add the onion mixture and tomato paste. Sauté for 1–2 minutes, then stir through the chicken pieces. Add the vinegar, brown sugar and water and bring to the boil. Simmer rapidly for about 8 minutes or until the sauce has thickened and the chicken is cooked through.

5　While the chicken is cooking, cut the lettuce into ½ cm strips. Slice the tomatoes and peel and slice the red onion into rounds. Place all the salad items on a platter ready for serving. Serve the chicken to the table with the salads, burritos or wraps, sour cream and cheese and everyone can build their own burrito.

FISH BURGERS

INGREDIENTS

Vegetable oil to fill pan to 5 mm (about 2 cups)

½ teaspoon salt

¼ teaspoon ground white pepper

½ cup plain flour

1 egg

1 cup fresh breadcrumbs

4 × 125 g boneless white fish fillets

4 soft white rolls (damper rolls are ideal)

250 g jar good-quality tartare sauce

50 g rocket

½ cup grated tasty cheese

EQUIPMENT

Chef pan

Cup and spoon measures

3 shallow dishes

Spoon

2 pairs of tongs

Egg flip

Fork

Paper towel

2 plates

1   Put the chef pan over a medium-high heat with the oil in it.

2   Add the salt and pepper to the flour in the first dish. In the second dish, beat the egg with 1 tablespoon of water. Place the breadcrumbs in the third dish.

3   Using tongs, dip a piece of fish into the flour and coat it completely, then dip it in the egg. Using a second pair of tongs, dip the fish into the crumb mixture, pressing the crumbs gently with your hands so they stick. Place the fish on a plate. Repeat with the remaining fish.

4   Lay each piece of fish in the frypan and fry for 3–4 minutes on each side or until golden brown and crunchy. Carefully remove with an egg flip onto a paper towel–lined plate.

5   To build the burgers, split the buns in half horizontally. Spread the tartare sauce on the bases and top with the rocket. Place the fish on top and sprinkle with the cheese. Cover with the top of the bun and serve immediately.

THREE-CHEESE QUESADILLAS

INGREDIENTS

1 cup grated tasty cheese

1 cup grated mozzarella cheese

½ cup ricotta

¼ cup olive oil + 2 teaspoons extra for dressing

8 soft white round wraps

50 g baby spinach

50 g rocket

½ cup tomato salsa

½ cup sour cream

EQUIPMENT

Food processor

Grill plate

2 mixing bowls, large and small

Chopping board

2 spoons

Wooden spoon

Tongs

Egg flip

Pastry brush

Pizza cutter

1 Heat the grill pan over a medium-high heat.

2 Place the 3 cheeses in the large mixing bowl and stir to combine.

3 Brush some oil on the grill plate. Place 2 wraps on the grill and top each with ¼ of the spinach, topped with ¼ of the cheese mixture. Spread to about 2 cm from the edge. Top each wrap with a second one and brush with oil. Press down hard with the egg flip to make sure the wraps are glued together. This should take 1–2 minutes. Using an egg flip (and tongs if necessary), carefully turn the whole round upside down and cook for a further minute. Remove to a chopping board and cut into 6 pieces with a pizza cutter.

4 Repeat with the next 4 wraps and filling. Divide the quesadillas between 4 plates.

5 Toss the rocket in the small mixing bowl with 2 teaspoons olive oil and divide between the 4 plates. Top with a dollop of salsa and sour cream, and serve.

GOURMET STEAK SANDWICH

INGREDIENTS

8 slices sourdough or rye bread

2 tablespoons olive oil

4 × 100 g thin cut scotch fillet steaks

¾ teaspoon salt

½ brown onion

½ cup whole-egg mayonnaise

1 tablespoon tomato sauce

1 tablespoon hot English mustard

2 teaspoons sugar

1 tablespoon gherkin relish

¼ baby cos lettuce

16 slices of dill pickles (bread and butter cucumbers)

EQUIPMENT

Mini food processor

Grill plate

Cup and spoon measures

Small mixing bowl

Chopping board

Knife

Spoon

Tongs

Pastry brush

Foil

Plate

1   Heat the grill plate over a high heat. Brush the bread with olive oil and place on the hot grill plate, one side only, until good char-marks appear. Remove and set aside. Brush the steak with oil and sprinkle some salt over. Cook for 1 minute on each side for medium rare. (Add 30–60 seconds each side for well done.) Remove from the grill and set aside under foil.

2   Peel and quarter the onion and place in the mini food processor. Blitz until finely minced. Place in the mixing bowl with the mayonnaise, tomato sauce, mustard, sugar, gherkin relish and ¼ teaspoon salt. Stir to combine. Separate the lettuce leaves.

3   To build the sandwich, place 4 slices of bread charred side down. Top each with ¼ of the dressing. Top with ¼ of the lettuce, then the pickles and the steak. Top with the other piece of bread, charred side up, and serve straight away.

NOTE › ASK YOUR BUTCHER TO CUT THIN SCOTCH FILLET STEAKS ESPECIALLY FOR YOU – THEY WILL BE MUCH NICER THAN THE USUAL MINUTE STEAKS AVAILABLE READY-CUT.

LAMB KOFTA PIZZA

INGREDIENTS

4 white tortillas

500 g lamb mince

1 teaspoon garlic powder

1 tablespoon ground coriander

1 tablespoon ground cumin

1 teaspoon salt

½ teaspoon ground black pepper

1 tablespoon olive oil

2 tablespoons pine nuts

½ cup plain Greek yoghurt

¼ cup thick mint sauce

½ red onion

50 g rocket

EQUIPMENT

Oven

2 large baking trays

Cup and spoon measures

2 mixing bowls, medium and small

2 chopping boards

Knife

Spoon

Pastry brush

Pizza cutter

Timer

Oven mitt

Baking paper

1 Preheat the oven to 200°C. Line the baking trays with baking paper and place 2 tortillas on each.

2 Put the lamb in the medium mixing bowl with the garlic powder, coriander, cumin, salt and pepper. Mix thoroughly using damp hands. Place ¼ of the mince mixture onto one of the tortillas. Still with damp hands, press the mince over the tortilla, spreading it to within a centimetre of the edges. Repeat with the remaining mince and tortillas. Brush a little oil around the edge of the tortillas and scatter the pine nuts over each pizza. Gently press them into the mince.

3 Put the trays in the oven for 3½ minutes. (Set the timer.) Swap the top and bottom trays and cook for a further 3½ minutes.

4 While the pizzas cook, combine the yoghurt and mint sauce in the small mixing bowl. Peel and finely slice the onion.

5 Remove the pizzas from the oven and place on a chopping board. Divide the rocket and sliced onion over the top of each one and drizzle with the yoghurt sauce. Cut each pizza in quarters with the pizza cutter and serve immediately.

CHICKEN WALDORF SALAD ON SOURDOUGH

INGREDIENTS

1 large chicken breast (about 300 g)

2 tablespoons olive oil

½ cup mayonnaise

¼ cup sour cream

2 tablespoons wholegrain mustard

Salt and ground white pepper

1 lemon

6 shallots

2 Granny Smith apples

2 celery stalks

100 g baby spinach

½ cup walnut pieces

4 slices sourdough bread

EQUIPMENT

Toaster

Chef pan

Cup and spoon measures

Large mixing bowl

2 chopping boards

Mandolin/V-slicer with julienne attachment

2 knives

Citrus squeezer

Spoon

Tongs

Meat mallet

Foil

Plate

1   Put the chef pan over a medium-high heat with 1 tablespoon of oil. Cut the chicken breast in half horizontally and hammer gently with a meat mallet to flatten it so that it is a uniform thickness (about 5 mm). Cook for about 3 minutes on each side, until golden brown and just cooked through. Remove to a plate and cover with foil.

2   In the large mixing bowl, combine the mayonnaise, sour cream, mustard and a pinch of salt and pepper. Squeeze the lemon in and stir to combine.

3   While the chicken is cooking, peel the shallots and slice ½ cm thick. Using the mandolin, julienne the unpeeled apples. Slice the celery in half lengthways and cut into 1 cm pieces. Place these into the mixing bowl with the dressing, along with the baby spinach and walnuts.

4   Put the bread into the toaster. Use the second chopping board to slice the chicken. Slice into 1 cm strips and toss through the salad.

5   Put a slice of toast on each of 4 plates and heap with the waldorf salad and serve.

STEAK BURRITOS

INGREDIENTS

1 teaspoon onion powder

1 teaspoon garlic powder

1 teaspoon smoky paprika

1 teaspoon ground cumin seeds

1 teaspoon ground coriander seeds

½ teaspoon ground dried chillies (optional)

1 teaspoon salt

600 g rump steak

Olive oil

½ iceberg lettuce

1 small red onion

1 jar salsa

½ cup sour cream

1 cup grated tasty cheese

8 soft flour tortillas

EQUIPMENT

Grill plate

Cup and spoon measures

Small mixing bowl

2 chopping boards

2 knives

Tongs

Foil

Plate

Serving bowls and platter

1 Heat the grill plate over a high heat. Place all the dry spices and salt in the small bowl and mix. Transfer to a plate. Dip the steak in the spice mixture to coat each side. When the grill is very hot, drizzle the steak with oil and cook on the grill for 2–3 minutes each side or until cooked to your liking. Remove from the grill to a chopping board and cover loosely with foil.

2 Chop the lettuce into pieces. Peel and halve the red onion, and slice. Place in serving bowls. Slice the steak and serve at the table with the accompaniments, cheese and tortillas, and let everyone build their own burritos.

HAM, AVOCADO AND PINEAPPLE PIZZA SUBS

INGREDIENTS

2 bake-at-home half-baguettes

½ cup barbecue sauce

25 g baby spinach

1 avocado

440 g tin crushed pineapple in juice

150 g shaved leg ham

½ cup grated tasty cheese

½ cup grated mozzarella cheese

EQUIPMENT

Oven

Cup measures

2 chopping boards

Wire rack

2 knives

Tin opener

Spoon

Oven mitt

1 Preheat the oven to 200°C.

2 Split the baguettes horizontally and place cut-side up on a wire rack. Divide the barbecue sauce between the 4 bases and spread with the back of a spoon to coat. Top with the baby spinach.

3 Halve the avocado and scoop the flesh out with a spoon. Roughly slice and scatter over the bases. Drain the pineapple well and divide between the bases. Give the shaved ham a rough chop and divide between the 4 bases. Put ¼ of each cheese over the top.

4 Place the wire rack directly onto an upper oven shelf. Bake for 8 minutes, or until the underside of the bread is toasty and the cheese is melted, bubbling and golden.

5 Remove from the oven and serve immediately.

NOTE › YOU COULD USE A STORE-BOUGHT TOMATO PIZZA SAUCE, IF YOU PREFER.

IN A
FLASH

SHARING DINNER WITH MY FAMILY IS THE HIGHLIGHT OF MY DAY, ESPECIALLY AS THEY ARE GROWING UP SO FAST AND ALREADY HAVE COMMITMENTS AND SOCIAL LIVES OF THEIR OWN. AFTER A BUSY DAY I AM MORE INTERESTED IN SITTING WITH THEM THAN I AM IN SPENDING HOURS GETTING DINNER READY.

QUICK PIES, FRITTERS, GRILLS AND SALADS ARE THE ORDER OF THE DAY IN THIS CHAPTER. THESE RECIPES ARE ABOUT REWORKING FAVOURITES TO COOK QUICKLY WITHOUT SACRIFICING QUALITY OR FLAVOUR, ALLOWING YOU MORE TIME TO SPEND WITH THE PEOPLE YOU LOVE.

RECIPES

SAVOURY MINCE PIE 198

BEEF SALAD WITH CRISPY NOODLES 201

VEGETARIAN SANG CHOY BOW 202

CORN CHOWDER 205

BAKED FISH WITH TOMATOES AND OLIVES 206

GREEK-STYLE LAMB CHOPS 209

PORTUGUESE-STYLE CHICKEN WITH CORN
AND PEA FRITTERS 210

GREEN CURRY CHICKEN PIE 213

VEGETABLE NOODLE FRITTATA 214

LAMB CHOPS WITH GARLIC SAUCE
AND COUSCOUS 217

BACON AND MUSHROOM FRITTATA

ON

INGREDIENTS

4 rashers bacon

6 medium or 12 small cup mushrooms

10 cherry tomatoes

6 fat shallots

8 eggs

½ cup milk

¼ teaspoon salt

¼ teaspoon ground white pepper

30 g baby spinach

1 cup grated tasty cheese

1 loaf Turkish bread

10 g rocket

1 tablespoon balsamic glaze

1 tablespoon extra virgin olive oil + ¼ cup
    for dipping bread

EQUIPMENT

Oven grill

28 cm oven-proof non-stick frypan

Cup and spoon measures

Bowl

2 chopping boards

2 knives

Spatula

Whisk

Oven mitt

2 dinner plates or platters (at least
    28 cm in diameter)

1   Preheat the oven grill to 200°C.

2   Place the frypan over a high heat. Strip the rind off the bacon and roughly chop. Quarter the mushrooms if they are medium, halve them if small. Put the bacon in the pan. When the fat starts to melt and coat the pan, add the mushrooms. Turn the heat down to medium and stir occasionally while you prepare the other vegetables.

3   Halve the cherry tomatoes. Peel the shallots and cut into 1 cm pieces.

4   Beat the eggs and milk together with a whisk. Add salt and pepper.

5   Put the tomatoes and shallots in the pan with the bacon and stir through. Pour in the egg mixture, and add the spinach and half the cheese. Stir with a spatula, lifting the egg from the bottom.

When the mixture is starting to thicken, arrange the ingredients so they are fairly evenly distributed over the base of the pan. Scatter the other half of the cheese over the top and place the pan on the bottom shelf of the oven.

6   Place the uncut Turkish bread on the bottom shelf also, just for a couple of minutes until it crisps. Slice into 3 cm wide strips.

7   When the frittata is golden brown, remove from the oven with an oven mitt (the handle will be hot). Put a plate over the top of the pan and invert to remove the frittata. Place a plate over the bottom of the frittata and invert again, so that it is right-side up. Top with the rocket, drizzle with balsamic glaze and a little oil, and serve to the table with the Turkish bread and extra olive oil for dipping.

BEEF TACOS

ON

INGREDIENTS

12 hard taco shells
2 garlic cloves
1 brown onion
2 tablespoons olive oil
2 teaspoons ground cumin seed
2 teaspoons smoked paprika
¼ teaspoon ground chilli
500 g beef mince
400 g tin chopped tomatoes
¼ iceberg lettuce
2 tomatoes
1 cup tomato salsa
1 cup grated tasty cheese
¾ cup sour cream

EQUIPMENT

Oven
Mini food processor
Chef pan
Baking tray
Cup and spoon measures
Chopping board
Knife
Spatula
Wooden spoon
Timer
Serving bowls and platter

1   Preheat the oven to 200°C. Spread the taco shells out on the tray. Set the timer for 10 minutes and place in the oven. When the timer goes off, remove from the oven and set aside.

2   While the taco shells warm, put the chef pan over a medium-high heat. Peel the garlic and peel and quarter the onion. Place in the mini food processor and blitz until finely chopped. Put the oil in the pan and cook the garlic and onion for a minute, stirring. Add the cumin, paprika, chilli and mince. Break up any lumps in the mince with the spoon. When the mince is browned, add the tomatoes and simmer.

3   While the beef cooks, cut the lettuce finely and put on a platter. Halve the tomatoes and remove the stalk end. Slice and add to the platter. Put the salsa, cheese and sour cream in bowls and place on the platter. Serve to the table with the taco shells and the mince, so everyone can build their own tacos.

CHICKEN FILLET WITH CREAMY LEEK AND BACON SAUCE

INGREDIENTS

8 chat potatoes (about 4 cm in diameter)

2 large skinless chicken breast fillets

1 tablespoon + 1 teaspoon olive oil

4 rashers bacon

1 leek

2 garlic cloves

Salt and ground white pepper

1 teaspoon plain flour

¼ cup white wine or stock

1 tablespoon Dijon mustard

½ cup thickened cream

EQUIPMENT

Chef pan

Medium frypan

Cup and spoon measures

2 chopping boards

2 knives

Wooden spoon

Tongs

Garlic crusher

Meat mallet

Foil

Plate

1 Place the potatoes around the edge of the microwave turntable and cook on high for 6–8 minutes.

2 Heat the chef pan over a medium-high heat. Cut the chicken breasts in half horizontally and hammer with a meat mallet to about 5 mm thick. Put a tablespoon of oil in the pan and add the chicken. Cook for around 3 minutes on each side, or until lightly golden on the outside and cooked through. Be careful not to overcook it. Set aside on a plate under foil.

3 Strip the rind off the bacon and cut into 1 cm pieces. Place in the hot pan, stirring occasionally. While the bacon is cooking, slice the white and pale green parts of the leek ½ cm thick. Add to the pan with the bacon. Crush the garlic into the pan. Sauté for 1–2 minutes or until the leek is softening.

4 Place the medium frypan over a high heat and add a teaspoon of olive oil. When the pan is hot put the microwaved potatoes in and toss so they have a little gloss and gain a little golden colour. Season with salt and pepper.

5 Sprinkle the flour over the leek mixture and stir through. Pour in the wine and cook for 1 minute. Add the Dijon mustard and cream. Bring to the boil, then turn the heat off. Taste and season with salt and pepper (bearing in mind that some bacon is very salty).

6 Serve the chicken with the sauce poured over the top, alongside the potatoes.

NOTE › THIS BACON AND LEEK SAUCE IS LOVELY ON PASTA AS WELL.

EGGS IN EGGPLANT RAGOUT

INGREDIENTS

1 tablespoon olive oil

2 cloves garlic

1 brown onion

1 eggplant

2 × 400 g tins chopped tomatoes

1 teaspoon salt

1 tablespoon sugar

2 tablespoons hot chilli sauce (optional)

8 eggs

40 g block of parmesan

2 tablespoons flat-leaf parsley

4 slices of bread or 2 rolls

Ground black pepper

EQUIPMENT

Oven

Mini food processor

Toaster

Chef pan

Cup and spoon measures

Chopping board

Knife

Fine grater

Tin opener

Spoon

Wooden spoon

Vegetable peeler

Oven mitt

4 shallow pie or gratin dishes

1   Preheat the oven to 200°C.

2   Heat the chef pan over a medium-high heat with the oil in it. Peel the garlic and peel and quarter the onion. Put into the mini food processor and blitz until finely chopped. Peel the eggplant and cut it into 1 cm cubes. Place in the pan with the onion and garlic and stir for a minute until the onion is soft and translucent.

3   Add the tomatoes, salt and sugar (and chilli sauce if using), and simmer rapidly, stirring, for 5 minutes. The sauce will thicken and the flavours intensify. If the sauce becomes too thick, add a little water.

4   Divide the sauce between the 4 shallow pie or gratin dishes. Make two little wells in each with a spoon and crack two eggs into the wells. Spoon a little of the tomato sauce over the egg whites. Grate a little parmesan over the top.

5   Place the dishes in the oven and bake for 6–8 minutes or until the whites of the eggs are set but the yolks are still runny.

6   While the eggs are cooking, grate the remaining parmesan and pick the parsley leaves from the stalks. Place the bread or rolls into the toaster. Remove the eggs from the oven and sprinkle with some black pepper, parmesan and parsley. Serve to the table in the dishes with the toast or rolls.

FISH AND LEEK PIE

INGREDIENTS

1 sheet frozen puff pastry

1 egg

50 g butter

2 leeks

¼ cup flour

2½ cups milk

1 tablespoon Dijon mustard

½ teaspoon salt

¼ teaspoon ground white pepper

500 g firm-fleshed white fish

EQUIPMENT

Oven

Chef pan

Baking tray

Cup and spoon measures

Small mixing bowl

2 chopping boards

Mandolin/V-slicer with plain attachment

2 knives

Big spoon

Wooden spoon

Pastry brush

Timer

Oven mitt

Fork

Baking paper

4 ramekins

1   Preheat the oven to 220°C.

2   Press a ramekin into the pastry sheet 4 times to create circles. Use a knife to cut around the circles. Place the circles on the lined baking tray. Beat the egg in the small bowl and brush onto the pastry. Place the tray on the centre shelf of the oven and set the timer for 15 minutes.

3   Put the chef pan over a medium heat with the butter in it. Slice the white and pale green parts of the leeks using the mandolin. Add to the pan and sauté for about 5 minutes or until soft. Add the flour and stir until well combined. Add the milk, ½ a cup at a time, stirring and ensuring that the flour cooks after each addition. Stir through the mustard and season with salt and pepper.

4   Cut the fish into 2 cm cubes and add to the pan. Turn the heat down and stir gently for 3–4 minutes or until cooked through. The sauce will seem quite thick at first, but the fish releases some juices as it cooks.

5   Remove the pastry from the oven. Spoon the mixture into the 4 ramekins. Top each ramekin with a pastry lid and serve.

PORK LARB

INGREDIENTS

¼ cup jasmine rice

1 tablespoon peanut or vegetable oil

500 g pork mince

½ bunch coriander

3 garlic cloves

1 red onion

1 long green chilli

¼ cup fish sauce

¼ cup brown sugar

2 limes

¼ bunch mint leaves

1 iceberg lettuce

1 cup bean sprouts

EQUIPMENT

Mini food processor

Chef pan

Cup and spoon measures

Small bowl

Chopping board

Knife

Fine grater

Citrus squeezer

Spatula

Wooden spoon

Teaspoon

1   Put the chef pan over a medium heat. Put the rice in the pan and toast for 2–3 minutes or until golden brown. Place the toasted rice in the mini food processor and blitz to a fine, gritty powder. Remove to a small bowl and set aside.

2   Put the oil in the pan. Add the pork mince and stir, using a wooden spoon to squash any lumps. Cook through.

3   While the pork is cooking, cut the roots and stems off the coriander. (It is important to rinse the stems thoroughly under running water as they can be very gritty.) Set the leaves aside for later, then trim any stringy bits off the roots and place with the stems in the mini food processor. Peel the garlic and peel and quarter the onion and place in the mini food processor.

Halve the chilli and scrape out the seeds with a teaspoon. Discard the seeds and stalk and place the chilli in the mini food processor. Blitz everything until finely chopped.

4   Add the coriander mixture to the pork in the pan and stir for 2–3 minutes until fragrant. Add the fish sauce and brown sugar. Zest the limes into the pan, then cut in half and squeeze in the juice. Remove the pan from the heat.

5   Pick the mint and coriander leaves onto a plate. Cut the lettuce in half. Remove the hard white core and separate the remaining leaves into cups.

6   Serve the larb mixture to the table with the bean sprouts, toasted rice, mint, coriander and lettuce and let everyone build their own.

COCK-A-LEEKIE SOUP

INGREDIENTS
1 tablespoon olive oil
4 chicken thigh fillets (about 400 g)
2 leeks
25 g butter
¼ cup flour
2 litres chicken stock
Salt and cracked black pepper
4 sourdough rolls, for serving

EQUIPMENT
Chef pan
Cup and spoon measures
2 chopping boards
Mandolin/V-slicer with plain attachment
2 knives
Wooden spoon
Tongs
Ladle

1 Put the chef pan over a medium-high heat and add the oil.

2 Cut the chicken into strips, about 6–8 pieces each. Put into the pan.

3 Use the mandolin to finely slice the white and pale green parts of the leeks. Add the butter to the pan, then the leeks. Stir for 3–4 minutes or until the leeks soften and collapse.

4 Sprinkle the flour over the contents of the pan and stir. Add a cup of stock and stir until the mixture thickens. Add another cup and repeat. Add the rest of the stock and bring to the boil.

5 Cook, stirring frequently, for another 5 minutes or until the chicken is cooked. Taste and season with salt and pepper. Ladle into bowls and serve with the sourdough rolls.

SMOKED SALMON AND ASPARAGUS FRITTATA WITH WARM POTATO SALAD

INGREDIENTS

8 small chat potatoes (about 4 cm in diameter)

1 teaspoon olive oil

6 shallots

1 bunch asparagus (preferably young, thin spears)

100 g smoked salmon

8 eggs

½ cup milk

¼ teaspoon salt

¼ teaspoon ground white pepper

1 cup grated mozzarella cheese

½ bunch dill

¼ cup sour cream

¼ cup whole-egg mayonnaise

1 tablespoon wholegrain mustard

1 lemon

EQUIPMENT

Oven grill

Microwave

28 cm oven-proof non-stick frypan

Cup and spoon measures

2 mixing bowls, large and medium

2 cutting boards

2 knives

Spatula

Whisk

Oven mitt

Fork

2 dinner plates or platters (at least 28 cm in diameter)

1 Preheat the oven grill to 200°C.

2 Place the chat potatoes in the microwave on high for 6 minutes.

3 Place the frypan over a medium heat with the oil in it. Peel the shallots and slice about 1 cm thick. Cut the asparagus diagonally into 3 cm lengths. Put them in the pan and sauté for one minute.

4 Cut the smoked salmon roughly into 3 cm strips. In the medium mixing bowl, beat the eggs and milk together with a whisk. Add the salt and pepper. Pour into the pan, add the salmon and half the mozzarella. Tear a few dill leaves into the pan and stir with a spatula, lifting the egg from the bottom. When the mixture is starting to thicken, arrange the ingredients so they are fairly evenly distributed over the base of the pan. Scatter the other half of the mozzarella over the top and put the pan on the bottom shelf of the oven.

5 While the frittata cooks, remove the potatoes from the microwave and cut into halves. In the large mixing bowl, combine the sour cream, mayonnaise and mustard. Chop the remaining dill leaves and stir through, along with the halved potatoes.

6 Cut the lemon into wedges.

7 After about 6 minutes the frittata will be golden brown on top and just set in the middle. Remove from the oven using a mitt as the handle will be very hot. Put a plate over the top of the pan and invert to remove the frittata. Place a plate over the bottom of the frittata and invert again, so that it is right-side up. Serve to the table with the lemon wedges and warm potato salad.

CHORIZO, HALOUMI AND POTATO SALAD

INGREDIENTS

8 chat potatoes (about 4 cm in diameter)
2 chorizo sausages
1 red onion
¼ cup olive oil
1 green capsicum
16 green beans
½ teaspoon sea salt flakes
125 g haloumi
¼ cup red wine vinegar
2 tablespoons wholegrain mustard
80 g baby rocket

EQUIPMENT

Chef pan
Cup and spoon measures
Large mixing bowl
2 chopping boards
2 knives
Wooden spoon
Tongs
Fork
Salad bowl

1 Place the potatoes around the edge of the microwave turntable and cook on high for 6 minutes.

2 Put the chef pan over a medium-high heat. Slice the chorizo ½ cm thick. Place in the chef pan for a minute or two until it becomes golden on one side. Turn and cook on the other side. Remove to the mixing bowl.

3 While the chorizo cooks, peel the onion and cut into wedges. Place a teaspoon of olive oil in the chef pan and add the onion. Cut the 4 sides and the base from the green capsicum and discard the seeds and stalk. Cut into wide strips and add to the pan. Cut the tops off the green beans and halve. Add to the pan as well. Sauté all the vegetables for 2–3 minutes or until the onion is soft and the beans tender but still crisp. Remove from the pan and place in the bowl with the chorizo.

4 Remove the potatoes from the microwave and cut in half. Put a tablespoon of olive oil in the pan and cook the potatoes cut-side down for 1–2 minutes or until golden. Remove, season with salt, and add to the mixing bowl.

5 Slice the haloumi into 3 cm long and ½ cm thick pieces. Lay it in the hot pan. Turn it after about 30 seconds – it should be golden. Turn and cook for another 30 seconds. Remove to the bowl with the other ingredients.

6 In the salad bowl, whisk together the remaining olive oil, red wine vinegar and wholegrain mustard. Add the rocket to the salad bowl, along with the contents of the mixing bowl. Gently toss the salad together and serve.

NOTE › BUY THE CHORIZO FROM THE DELI, NOT THE KIND YOU BUY IN THE SAUSAGE SECTION OF THE BUTCHER'S.

GARLIC PARSLEY MUSSELS

INGREDIENTS

6 cloves garlic

2 long red chillies

8 shallots

40 g butter

1 kg live pot-ready mussels

½ cup white wine

½ cup chicken or fish stock

1 baguette

½ bunch flat-leaf parsley

EQUIPMENT

Mini food processor

Chef pan with lid

Cup measures

Chopping board

Knife

Bread knife

Wooden spoon

Teaspoon

1   Peel the garlic and place in the mini food processor. Halve the chillies lengthways and scrape out the seeds with a teaspoon. Discard the seeds and stalks. Place in the mini food processor with the garlic and blitz until finely chopped. Peel the shallots and slice diagonally.

2   Heat the chef pan over a medium-low heat and melt the butter. Add the garlic and chilli mixture and the shallots. Sauté for a minute or two until everything softens but does not brown.

3   Turn the heat up to medium high and add the mussels, wine and stock. Put the lid on the pan and bring to the boil. Turn the heat down and simmer for 6–8 minutes. Most (if not all) of the mussels will open – throw away any that don't.

4   While the mussels cook, cut the baguette into big chunks. Pick the parsley leaves off the stalks.

5   Remove the pan from the heat. Toss through the parsley, and serve at the table in the pan along with the bread to mop up the delicious broth.

NOTE › POT-READY LIVE MUSSELS ARE SCRUBBED AND BEARDED. THEY ARE READY IN VAC-SEALED BAGS FROM THE FISHMONGER.

ZUCCHINI FRITTERS

INGREDIENTS

4 rashers bacon

3 zucchini

1 red onion

½ cup grated tasty cheese

¾ cup self-raising flour

¼ teaspoon salt

¼ teaspoon ground white pepper

3 eggs

½ cup milk

2 tablespoon olive oil

125 g tomato relish

EQUIPMENT

Chef pan

Cup and spoon measures

Large measuring jug

Large mixing bowl

2 chopping boards

2 knives

Spoon

Wooden spoon

Egg flip

Whisk

Grater

Foil

Paper towel

Plate

1   Put the chef pan over a medium-high heat. Strip the rind off the bacon and discard. Cut the bacon into thirds and put in the pan. Cook for a couple of minutes on each side, until golden and crisp. When it is done, remove from the pan and put on a plate with paper towel, and cover loosely with foil. Reduce the heat to medium.

2   While the bacon is cooking, grate the zucchini into the large mixing bowl. Peel the onion and grate it into the bowl as well. Add the cheese. Sprinkle the flour, salt and pepper over and stir to mix. Beat the eggs and milk together in the measuring jug, then add to the bowl and stir through with a wooden spoon.

3   Add a tablespoon of olive oil to the pan and dollop large spoonfuls of the mixture in You should be able to fit 6 fritters in the pan, using about half the mixture. Cook for 2 minutes or until golden underneath. Flip and cook for another 1–2 minutes. Remove and put under foil with the bacon. Repeat with the remaining oil and mixture.

4   Serve the fritters with bacon on top and a good dollop of tomato relish.

SPINACH AND FETA FRITTATA

ON

INGREDIENTS

1 teaspoon + 1 tablespoon olive oil

8 shallots

8 eggs

½ cup milk

Salt and ground black pepper

100 g baby spinach

100 g feta

1 cup grated tasty cheese

1 lemon

1 punnet grape tomatoes

1 Lebanese cucumber

12 pitted kalamata olives

4 dinner rolls, to serve

EQUIPMENT

Oven grill

28 cm oven-proof non-stick frypan

Cup and spoon measures

2 mixing bowls, large and medium

Chopping board

Knife

Citrus squeezer

Spatula

Tongs

Whisk

Oven mitt

Fork

2 dinner plates or platters (at least
   28 cm in diameter)

1 Preheat the oven grill to 200°C.

2 Place the frypan over medium heat with the teaspoon of oil in it. Peel the shallots and slice about 1 cm thick. Put half the shallots in the pan and sauté for one minute, reserving the rest for the salad.

3 In the medium mixing bowl, beat the eggs and milk together with a whisk. Add ¼ teaspoon each of salt and pepper. Pour into the pan, add the spinach and crumble through the feta. Add half the grated tasty cheese and stir with a spatula, lifting the egg from the bottom. When the mixture is starting to thicken, arrange the ingredients so they are fairly evenly distributed over the base of the pan. Scatter the other half of the cheese over the top and put the pan on the bottom shelf of the oven.

4 While the frittata cooks, put the tablespoon of olive oil in the large mixing bowl. Squeeze half the lemon in and whisk with a fork. Place the grape tomatoes in the bowl. Quarter the cucumber lengthways and cut into 1 cm lengths. Add to the bowl along with the olives and shallots. Season with salt and pepper and toss to mix.

5 After about 6 minutes the frittata will be golden brown on top and just set in the middle. Remove from the oven using a mitt as the handle will be very hot. Put a plate over the top of the pan and invert to remove the frittata. Place a plate over the bottom of the frittata and invert again, so that it is right-side up. Serve to the table with bread rolls and salad.

THESE RECIPES ARE ABOUT REWORKING
FAVOURITES TO COOK QUICKLY WITHOUT
SACRIFICING QUALITY OR FLAVOUR.

20|20

SAVOURY MINCE PIE

INGREDIENTS

1 sheet frozen puff pastry

1 egg

1 teaspoon vegetable oil

500 g beef mince

2 small brown onions

3 celery stalks

2 medium carrots

½ cup tomato paste

¼ cup plain flour

1 cup beef stock

Salt and pepper

EQUIPMENT

Oven

Food processor

Chef pan

Baking tray

Cup and spoon measures

Small mixing bowl

Chopping board

2 knives

Big spoon

Wooden spoon

Vegetable peeler

Pastry brush

Timer

Oven mitt

Fork

Baking paper

4 ramekins

1 Preheat the oven to 220°C.

2 Press a ramekin into the pastry sheet 4 times to create circles. Use a knife to cut around the circles. Place the circles on the lined baking tray. Beat the egg in the small bowl and brush onto the pastry. Place the tray on the centre shelf of the oven and set the timer for 15 minutes.

3 Put the chef pan over a medium-high heat with the oil in it. Put the mince in the pan and cook for 5 minutes until starting to brown.

4 Peel and halve the onions and place in the food processor. Cut the celery roughly into 4 cm lengths and add. Peel the carrots, cut into chunks and add. Blitz until chopped. Add to the mince and cook, stirring to break up any lumps in the mince. Cook for about 7 minutes or until the vegetables are soft and fragrant.

5 Add the tomato paste and sauté for a further minute. Sprinkle the flour over the meat mixture and stir to mix through. Add the stock a little at a time until it has all been incorporated. If the mixture is too thick, add a little water. The meat mixture should be a lovely dark reddish-brown colour, and the gravy will be rich. Taste, and season with salt and pepper.

6 Remove the pastry from the oven. Spoon the mixture into the 4 ramekins. Top each ramekin with a pastry lid and serve.

BEEF SALAD WITH CRISPY NOODLES

INGREDIENTS

½ cup white sugar

½ cup white vinegar

1 clove garlic

1 small red chilli

⅓ cup fish sauce

1 tablespoon peanut or vegetable oil

500 g rump steak

Salt

¼ wombok (Chinese cabbage)

4 shallots

1 Lebanese cucumber

1 carrot

⅓ bunch mint

⅓ bunch coriander

100 g packet of Chang's crunchy fried noodles

EQUIPMENT

Mini food processor

Chef pan

Medium pot

Cup and spoon measures

Large mixing bowl

2 chopping boards

Mandolin/V-slicer with julienne attachment

2 knives

Wooden spoon

Teaspoon

Tongs

Foil

Plate

1   Put the chef pan over a high heat.

2   Combine the sugar and vinegar in a medium pot over a medium-high heat. Stir until the sugar dissolves. Bring to the boil and boil for 5 minutes or until slightly thickened. While it is cooking, place the garlic and chilli in the mini food processor and blitz until finely chopped. Remove the dressing from the heat and add the fish sauce. Cool for a few minutes then add the garlic and chilli. Set aside.

3   Put the oil in the pan. Season the steak with salt and cook for 2 minutes on each side (or longer, if the steak is thick or you like it more well done). Remove from the pan and set aside on a plate under foil to rest.

4   While the meat cooks, get on with the vegetables. Slice the wombok thinly with a knife. Peel and chop the shallots. Halve the cucumber lengthways and scoop out the seeds with a teaspoon. Use the mandolin to julienne the cucumber and carrot. Put them in the large bowl with the wombok and shallots. Pick the leaves from the mint and coriander and add to the bowl.

5   Slice the rump steak and add it to the salad bowl along with the noodles. Pour over the dressing, toss through, and serve straight away.

VEGETARIAN SANG CHOY BOW

INGREDIENTS

2 tablespoons peanut or vegetable oil

750 g button mushrooms

2 garlic cloves

1 brown onion

225 g tin bamboo shoots

225 g tin water chestnuts

2 teaspoons cornflour

¼ cup oyster sauce

2 tablespoons soy sauce

½ iceberg lettuce

6 shallots

¼ bunch coriander

1 cup bean sprouts

¼ cup crispy fried shallots

EQUIPMENT

Food processor

Chef pan

Cup and spoon measures

Chopping board

Knife

Tin opener

Wooden spoon

Serving platter

1 Put the chef pan over a medium-high heat with the oil in it. Place the mushrooms in the food processor and blitz to a fine dice. Tip into the hot pan.

2 Peel the garlic and peel and quarter the onion. Place in the food processor and blitz until finely chopped. Add to the mushrooms in the pan and stir. Drain the tinned bamboo shoots and water chestnuts. Place in the food processor and blitz until roughly chopped. Add to the pan.

3 Cook, stirring occasionally, for about 5 minutes. The mushrooms will release moisture, which will then evaporate. When this happens, sprinkle the cornflour over the mixture and add ¼ cup water. Add the oyster sauce and soy sauce and cook for a couple more minutes, until the cornflour has cooked and the mixture is dark and glossy.

4 While the mushroom mixture cooks, separate out the lettuce leaves and put on a platter on the table. Peel and slice the shallots. Pick the leaves off the coriander and place on a platter with the bean sprouts, shallots and the crispy fried shallots.

5 Serve the mushrooms at the table in the pan. Let everyone build their own by putting some mushrooms into the lettuce, then topping with bean sprouts, shallots, coriander leaves and a few crispy shallots.

CORN CHOWDER

INGREDIENTS

4 cobs corn

1 tablespoon olive oil

4 rashers bacon

1 brown onion

4 medium sebago potatoes (about 700 g)

1 litre chicken stock

1 shallot

4 slices sourdough bread

½ cup cream

Salt and finely ground white pepper

Butter

EQUIPMENT

Food processor

Toaster

Kettle

Hand-held stick mixer

Large pot with lid

Cup and spoon measures

Small mixing bowl

2 chopping boards

2 knives

Wooden spoon

Plate

1 Remove the husks from the corn and lay on a plate. Microwave on high for 6 minutes, or until tender. Remove from the microwave and remove the kernels by running the knife down the cob.

2 While the corn cooks, place the large pot over a medium-high heat and add the olive oil. Strip the rind from the bacon and discard. Cut the bacon into strips and add it to the pot, stirring for a couple of minutes until light golden brown. Remove from the pot. Half-fill the kettle with water and boil.

3 Peel and halve the onion and potatoes and place in the food processor. Blitz until roughly chopped. Add the mixture to the pot and sauté for 2 minutes or until starting to soften. Add the chicken stock and 1 cup of boiling water. Turn the heat up to high, put the lid on the pot and bring to the boil. Remove the lid and boil for 6 minutes or until the potato is completely tender. Remove the pot from the heat and add half the corn kernels.

4 While the soup is simmering, peel and slice the shallot. Put the bread into the toaster.

5 Using a hand-held stick mixer, puree the soup until smooth. Add the cream, then taste and season with salt and pepper. Add almost all the bacon and remaining corn kernels, reserving a few to garnish. Serve topped with corn kernels, bacon and shallots, with buttered toast on the side.

BAKED FISH WITH TOMATOES AND OLIVES

INGREDIENTS

2 lemons

4 × 120 g skinless, boneless white fish fillets

½ punnet grape tomatoes

16 pitted kalamata olives

3 cloves garlic

20 g butter

2 tablespoons olive oil

2 tins cannellini beans

¼ teaspoon salt

¼ teaspoon cracked white pepper

¼ bunch flat-leaf parsley

EQUIPMENT

Oven

Food processor

Medium pot

Baking tray

Spoon measures

Small mixing bowl

Chopping board

Colander

Knife

Fine grater

Tin opener

Spatula

Egg flip

Garlic crusher

Kitchen scissors

Oven mitt

Baking paper

Foil

1　Preheat the oven to 200°C.

2　Lay a 50 cm length of foil on the benchtop and lay a slightly shorter piece of baking paper over the top.

3　Zest one of the lemons into a small mixing bowl. Slice into ½ cm thick slices and lay in a row in the middle of the baking paper. Place the pieces of fish on top. Place the grape tomatoes and olives in the bowl with the lemon zest. Crush 2 cloves of garlic into the bowl and mix together. Scatter this mixture over the fish pieces and drizzle with oil. Draw the top and bottom edges of the foil up into the middle, scrunching it together to form a tent. Roll the ends up to seal the parcel. Lift from the top onto a baking tray and place in the oven for 10 minutes.

4　While the fish cooks, place the pot over a medium heat with the butter and olive oil in it. Crush the remaining garlic into the pot. Tip the beans into the colander and rinse under the tap. Place them in the food processor and blitz until smooth. Add water, a little at a time, until a smooth puree consistency is achieved. Tip the bean puree into the pot and heat through. Taste and season with salt and ground white pepper. Cut the remaining lemon into wedges.

5　Remove the fish from the oven. Serve the bean puree with the fish on top, drizzled with the contents of the parcel. Using the kitchen scissors, snip the parsley leaves generously over the fish and serve with a lemon wedge.

GREEK-STYLE LAMB CHOPS

INGREDIENTS

1 teaspoon garlic powder

1 teaspoon salt

¼ teaspoon ground black pepper

8 mid loin lamb chops (about 700 g)

¼ cup olive oil + 1 tablespoon extra for drizzling

1 zucchini

1 red capsicum

2 red onions

2 tablespoons red wine vinegar

1 teaspoon sea salt flakes

50 g rocket

50 g feta

EQUIPMENT

Grill plate

Cup and spoon measures

2 mixing bowls, large and small

Chopping board

Knife

Tongs

Whisk

Foil

Plate

Serving platter

1 Put the grill plate over a high heat. In the small mixing bowl, combine the garlic powder, salt and pepper. Drizzle the chops with a little olive oil and sprinkle with the salt mixture. Cook the chops for about 4 minutes each side, turning once. They should be lovely and charred on the outside but still a bit pink in the middle. This depends on preference of course, as well as the thickness of the chops. Once cooked, place on a plate under foil to rest.

2 While the chops are cooking, prepare the vegetables. Cut the zucchini into 1 cm thick slices. Cut the 4 sides and the base off the capsicum and cut into 2 cm squares. Peel the onions and cut into 1 cm wedges. Drizzle all the vegetables with olive oil.

3 Place the oiled vegetables on the grill and cook for 1–2 minutes. Turn and cook the other side for a further minute or two, until the vegetables have char-marks and are tender but not too soft.

4 In the large mixing bowl, whisk together the remaining olive oil with the red wine vinegar and sea salt flakes. Toss through the chargrilled vegetables and rocket. Place on a platter with the feta crumbled over the top and serve with the lamb.

NOTE › THIS DISH CAN BE COOKED ON THE BARBECUE, BUT IT WILL NEED TO BE PREHEATED, WHICH IS NOT INCLUDED IN THE 20 MINUTES' COOKING TIME.

PORTUGUESE-STYLE CHICKEN WITH CORN AND PEA FRITTERS

INGREDIENTS

1 teaspoon sweet paprika

1 teaspoon chilli powder

1 teaspoon ground cinnamon

1 teaspoon garlic powder

1 teaspoon onion powder

1 teaspoon salt

2 large chicken breast fillets (about 600 g)

⅓ cup olive oil

4 shallots

400 g tin sweet corn kernels

2 eggs

⅓ cup milk

¾ cup self-raising flour

1 cup frozen baby peas

Salt and ground white pepper

1 lemon

EQUIPMENT

Chef pan

Grill plate

Cup and spoon measures

3 mixing bowls, large, medium and small

2 chopping boards

2 knives

Tin opener

Wooden spoon

Tongs

Egg flip

Meat mallet

Whisk

Plate

1 Put the grill plate over a medium-high heat and the chef pan over a medium-low heat.

2 Combine all the dry spices and the teaspoon of salt in the small mixing bowl and tip onto a plate. Cut the chicken in half horizontally and pound gently with the meat mallet to an even thickness (about 5 mm). Dip each side of the chicken into the spice mix.

3 Drizzle the chicken with oil and place on the grill and cook for about 3 minutes each side, or until lightly golden and cooked through. Remove from grill and set aside to rest.

4 While the chicken is cooking, peel and slice the shallots and drain the corn kernels. Whisk the eggs and milk together in the medium mixing bowl. Place the flour in the large mixing bowl and add the milk mixture gradually, whisking to ensure there are no lumps.

5 Stir in the corn kernels, peas and shallots, and a pinch of salt and pepper. Drizzle some olive oil in the chef pan. Drop spoonfuls of the fritter mix in the pan. Give the fritters space to spread and yourself space to flip them. After about 2 minutes, they will start setting on the edges of the upper surface, and be golden brown underneath. Flip and cook for another minute. While the fritters cook, cut the lemon into 8 wedges.

6 Serve the chicken and fritters with lemon wedges.

GREEN CURRY CHICKEN PIE

INGREDIENTS

1 sheet frozen puff pastry

1 egg

1 tablespoon peanut oil

500 g chicken thigh fillets

1 red onion

1 garlic clove

¼ cup green curry paste

1 zucchini

2 tablespoons flour

400 ml tin coconut milk

2 tablespoons brown sugar

2 tablespoons fish sauce

1 lime

EQUIPMENT

Oven

Chef pan

Baking tray

Cup and spoon measures

Small mixing bowl

2 chopping boards

2 knives

Citrus squeezer

Big spoon

Wooden spoon

Tongs

Garlic crusher

Pastry brush

Timer

Oven mitt

Fork

Baking paper

4 ramekins

1 Preheat the oven to 220°C.

2 Press a ramekin into the pastry sheet 4 times to create circles. Use a knife to cut around the circles. Place the circles on the lined baking tray. Beat the egg in the small bowl and brush onto the pastry. Place the tray on the centre shelf of the oven and set the timer for 15 minutes.

3 Put the chef pan over a medium-high heat with the oil in it. Cut the chicken thighs into cubes, about 8 pieces each. Place the chicken in the pan.

4 Peel, halve and roughly chop the onion. Place in the pan. Crush the garlic into the pan. Add the green curry paste and stir through. Cook for a further minute.

5 Quarter the zucchini lengthways and cut into 1 cm chunks. Add to the pan. Sprinkle the flour over the pan and stir to mix. Add the coconut milk and bring to the boil. Simmer for about 5 minutes, until the chicken is cooked through and the zucchini is tender. Remove from the heat and add the sugar and fish sauce. Squeeze the lime into the pan. Taste and see if you would prefer more sugar or fish sauce.

6 Remove the pastry from the oven. Spoon the mixture into the 4 ramekins. Top each ramekin with a pastry lid and serve.

VEGETABLE NOODLE FRITTATA

INGREDIENTS

200 g packet shelf-fresh Hokkien noodles

1 carrot

1 red capsicum

1 zucchini

2 tablespoons peanut or vegetable oil

2 garlic cloves

⅓ cup hoisin sauce

2 tablespoons light soy sauce

8 large eggs

4 shallots

2 tablespoons kecap manis (sweetened soy sauce)

1 cup bean sprouts

Ground white pepper

2 tablespoons crispy fried shallots

EQUIPMENT

Oven

Kettle

28 cm oven-proof non-stick frypan

Cup and spoon measures

Bowl

Medium mixing bowl

Chopping board

Colander

Mandolin/V-slicer with julienne attachment

Knife

Spatula

Wooden spoon

Vegetable peeler

Garlic crusher

Whisk

Oven mitt

1 Preheat the oven to 200°C.

2 Boil the kettle. Put the noodles in a bowl and pour boiling water over them. Let stand for a minute before straining through the colander.

3 Put the frypan over a medium-high heat. Peel the carrot and slice into a julienne with the mandolin. Also using the mandolin, slice the capsicum and zucchini. Place the oil in the pan. Add the vegetables and crush the garlic into the pan. Stir-fry for one minute, then add the hoisin and soy sauces. Add the noodles to the pan and turn the heat down to low.

4 In the mixing bowl, beat the eggs with ½ cup water. Pour into the pan and stir with a spatula, lifting the egg from the bottom. When the mixture is starting to thicken, arrange the ingredients so they are fairly evenly distributed over the base of the pan. Put the pan in the oven.

5 While the frittata cooks, peel and slice the shallots.

6 After about 6 minutes the frittata will be just set in the middle. Remove from the oven using a mitt as the handle will be very hot. Drizzle the kecap manis over the top, and top with bean sprouts, shallots, pepper and crispy fried shallots. Serve to the table in the pan.

LAMB CHOPS WITH GARLIC SAUCE AND COUSCOUS

INGREDIENTS

8 mid loin lamb chops (about 700 g)

3 tablespoons olive oil

Salt and ground black pepper

¾ cup instant couscous

¼ bunch flat-leaf parsley

1 red onion

½ punnet cherry tomatoes

2 lemons

3 garlic cloves

¾ cup neutral, light-flavoured oil (such as rice bran oil)

1 eggwhite

EQUIPMENT

Food processor

Kettle

Hand-held stick mixer

Grill plate

Tall, narrow jug or cup (the ones that come with most hand-held stick blenders are perfect)

Cup and spoon measures

Large mixing bowl

Chopping board

Knife

Citrus squeezer

Tongs

Fork

Foil

Plate

1 Put the grill plate over a high heat. Drizzle the chops with a tablespoon of olive oil and sprinkle with salt and pepper. Cook the chops for about 4 minutes each side, turning once. They should be lovely and charred on the outside but still a bit pink in the middle. This depends on preference, as well as the thickness of the chops. Once cooked, place on a plate under foil to rest.

2 Boil the kettle. Place the couscous in the large mixing bowl and add ¾ cup boiling water and the rest of the olive oil. Let stand for a few minutes. Twist the stalks off the parsley and discard. Place the leaves in the food processor. Peel and quarter the onion and add to the food processor. Blitz until roughly chopped. Fluff the couscous with a fork and add the parsley and onion. Halve the cherry tomatoes and add to the bowl. Squeeze over the juice of one lemon and stir to combine.

3 While the chops are resting, prepare the garlic sauce. Peel and halve the garlic cloves and place in the narrow jug with the juice of one lemon, the neutral oil, eggwhite and a pinch of salt. Place the stick mixer in the very bottom of the jug and turn it on. Leave the stick mixer going at the bottom of the cup until the mixture starts to turn white and fluffy. Slowly, draw the mixer upwards. By the time the stick mixer reaches the top, the mixture will be white, fluffy and ready to serve alongside the lamb chops and couscous.

JANUARY IN SEASON

FRUIT

Apricot	Peach
Banana	Pineapple
Blackberry	Plum
Blueberry	Raspberries
Cherry	Rockmelon
Grapes	Star fruit
Honeydew	Strawberry
Lychee	Tamarillo
Mango	Watermelon
Nectarine	

VEGETABLES & HERBS

Asparagus	Onion
Avocado	Oregano
Basil	Peas
Capsicum	Potato
Celery	Radish
Corn	Sage
Chives	Snow peas
Coriander	Spinach
Cucumber	Squash
Eggplant	Sugar snap peas
Garlic	Tarragon
Green beans	Thyme
Lettuce	Tomato
Mint	Zucchini

FEBRUARY IN SEASON

FRUIT

Banana
Blackberry
Blueberry
Fig
Grapes
Honeydew
Kiwifruit
Lemon
Lime
Lychee
Mango
Nectarine

Passionfruit
Peach
Pineapple
Plum
Raspberries
Rhubarb
Rockmelon
Star fruit
Strawberry
Tamarillo
Watermelon

VEGETABLES & HERBS

Basil
Capsicum
Celery
Chillies
Coriander
Corn
Cucumber
Eggplant
Fennel
Garlic
Green beans
Leek
Lemongrass
Lettuce

Mint
Onion
Oregano
Peas
Radish
Sage
Shallots (green/
    spring onions)
Snow peas
Squash
Sugar snap peas
Tarragon
Thyme
Zucchini

FRUIT

Banana	Passionfruit
Feijoa	Peach
Fig	Pear
Grapes	Persimmon
Guava	Pineapple
Honeydew	Plum
Kiwifruit	Pomegranate
Lemon	Quince
Lime	Rhubarb
Mandarin	Rockmelon
Mango	Strawberry
Orange	Tamarillo

VEGETABLES & HERBS

Beetroot	Onion
Broccoli	Oregano
Cabbage	Peas
Capsicum	Potato
Carrot	Pumpkin
Celery	Sage
Chilli	Shallots (green/ spring onions)
Coriander	
Cucumber	Silverbeet
Eggplant	Spinach
Fennel	Squash
Green beans	Sweet corn
Leek	Thyme
Lettuce	Tomato
Mint	Wombok
Mushrooms	Zucchini
Olive	

APRIL IN SEASON

FRUIT

Apple	Lime
Banana	Passionfruit
Custard apple	Pear
Fig	Persimmon
Grapes	Plum
Guava	Pomegranate
Honeydew	Quince
Kiwifruit	Rockmelon
Lemon	Tamarillo

VEGETABLES & HERBS

Asian greens	Mushrooms
Avocado	Olives
Beetroot	Onion
Broccoli	Oregano
Brussels sprouts	Parsnip
Cabbage	Peas
Capsicum	Potato
Carrot	Pumpkin
Celery	Sage
Chillies	Shallots (green/ spring onions)
Coriander	
Cucumber	Silverbeet
Eggplant	Spinach
Fennel	Squash
Garlic	Sweet corn
Ginger	Sweet potato
Green beans	Thyme
Leek	Tomato
Mint	Zucchini

MAY IN SEASON

FRUIT

Apples	Orange
Cumquat	Pear
Custard apple	Persimmon
Kiwifruit	Pomegranate
Lemon	Quince
Lime	Tamarillo

VEGETABLES & HERBS

Avocado	Parsnip
Beetroot	Potato
Brussels sprouts	Pumpkin
Carrot	Radicchio
Celeriac	Red cabbage
Celery	Shallots (green/
Eggplant	spring onions)
Endive	Silverbeet
Fennel	Spinach
Jerusalem artichoke	Sweet potato
Leek	Tomato
Lettuce	Witlof
Mushrooms	

JUNE IN SEASON

FRUIT

Apples
Cumquat
Custard apple
Kiwifruit
Lemon
Lime
Mandarin
Orange
Pear
Persimmon
Pomegranate
Quince
Tamarillo

VEGETABLES & HERBS

Avocado
Beetroot
Broad beans
Broccoli
Brussels sprouts
Carrot
Cauliflower
Celeriac
Celery
Eggplant
Endive
Fennel
Jerusalem artichoke
Leek
Lettuce
Mushrooms
Parsnip
Potato
Pumpkin
Radicchio
Red cabbage
Shallots (green/
   spring onions)
Silverbeet
Spinach
Sweet potato
Witlof

JULY IN SEASON

FRUIT

Apple	Nashi
Avocado	Orange
Custard apple	Papaya
Grapefruit	Pineapple
Kiwifruit	Pomegranate
Lemon	Quince
Lime	Rhubarb
Mandarin	

VEGETABLES & HERBS

Artichoke	Horseradish
Avocado	Jerusalem artichoke
Beetroot	Kale
Bok choy	Leek
Broccoli	Olive
Broccolini	Onion
Brown onion	Parsnip
Brussels sprouts	Potato
Cabbage	Pumpkin
Carrot	Shallots (green/
Cauliflower	spring onions)
Celeriac	Silverbeet
Celery	Spinach
Chinese greens	Swede
Dutch carrots	Sweet potato
Fennel	Turnip
Garlic	Witlof
Ginger	

AUGUST IN SEASON

FRUIT

Apple	Mandarin
Cumquat	Orange
Grapefruit	Pear
Lemon	Pineapple
Lime	

VEGETABLES & HERBS

Artichoke	Horseradish
Avocado	Leek
Beetroot	Okra
Bok choy	Olive
Broccoli	Onion
Cabbage	Parsnip
Carrot	Potato
Cauliflower	Pumpkin
Celeriac	Shallots (green/
Celery	spring onions)
Chinese broccoli	Silverbeet
Fennel	Spinach
Garlic	Turnip
Ginger	Witlof

SEPTEMBER IN SEASON

FRUIT

Apple	Orange
Blood orange	Pineapple
Grapefruit	Rockmelon
Lemon	Strawberry
Mandarin	Tangelo

VEGETABLES & HERBS

Artichoke	Green asparagus
Asparagus	Green beans
Avocado	Leek
Basil	Lettuce
Beetroot	Mint
Bok choy	Mushrooms
Broad beans	Onion
Broccoli	Oregano
Cabbage	Peas
Carrot	Potato
Cauliflower	Pumpkin
Chillies	Silverbeet
Chinese broccoli	Spinach
Chinese greens	Shallots (green/
Chives	spring onions)
Eggplant	Thyme
Garlic	Zucchini
Ginger	

OCTOBER IN SEASON

FRUIT

Banana	Passionfruit
Blueberry	Papaya
Grapefruit	Pineapple
Lemon	Rockmelon
Mango	Strawberry
Orange	Tangelo

VEGETABLES & HERBS

Artichoke	Lemongrass
Asparagus	Lettuce
Avocado	Mint
Basil	Mushrooms
Beetroot	Onion
Bok choy	Oregano
Broad beans	Peas
Broccoli	Potato
Chives	Sage
Coriander	Silverbeet
Cucumber	Spinach
Eggplant	Shallots (green/
Garlic	spring onions)
Ginger	Thyme
Green beans	Zucchini

NOVEMBER IN SEASON

FRUIT

Banana	Orange
Blueberry	Passionfruit
Cherry	Pineapple
Grapefruit	Rhubarb
Honeydew	Rockmelon
Lemon	Strawberry
Lychee	Watermelon
Mango	

VEGETABLES & HERBS

Artichoke	Marjoram
Asparagus	Mint
Avocado	Onion
Basil	Oregano
Beetroot	Peas
Broccoli	Sage
Corn	Silverbeet
Cucumber	Spinach
Chervil	Shallots (green/
Coriander	spring onions)
Eggplant	Tarragon
Garlic	Thyme
Green beans	Zucchini
Lettuce	

DECEMBER IN SEASON

FRUIT

Banana	Mango
Blueberry	Papaya
Cherry	Pineapple
Grapefruit	Rockmelon
Honeydew	Strawberry
Lemon	Watermelon
Lychee	

VEGETABLES & HERBS

Artichoke	Garlic
Asparagus	Green beans
Avocado	Lettuce
Basil	Mint
Beetroot	Onion
Broccoli	Oregano
Corn	Peas
Chives	Potatoes
Coriander	Silverbeet
Cucumber	Spinach
Dill	Sugar snap peas
Eggplant	Zucchini

INDEX

NOTES

NOTES

NOTES

NOTES

NOTES

NOTES

NOTES

julie's place

I have always loved sharing food with people and am constantly on the lookout for the opportunity to gather people together for a meal. In the past it's been my great pleasure to share my cooking with my family and friends. Since *MasterChef*, I have been so privileged to be able to share my cooking through my recipes.

I am now so thrilled to have opened Julie's Place on the Central Coast. Julie's Place hosts cookery classes, corporate team days, and special events. I sincerely hope I have created a warm and welcoming place where people will gather, cook together, learn something, and then enjoy the food that we have made.

I'm over the moon about this new chapter in my life. I do hope you'll come along and share it with me.

www.juliesplace.com.au

Follow Julie online:

juliegoodwin.com.au
facebook.com/juliegoodwincooklivelove
twitter.com/_JulieGoodwin

ACKNOWLEDGEMENTS

I would like to acknowledge the vision, creativity and commitment of the team who have brought *20/20 Meals* to life: publisher Robert Watkins, in-house editor Karen Ward, and the whole team at Hachette Australia; designer Liz Seymour; editor Elizabeth Cowell; proofreader Susin Chow; photographer Steve Brown; home economist Tracey Meharg; and food stylist Trish Heagerty.

I would like to acknowledge the generosity of GLAD, Howards Storage World and Le Creuset.

I would like to thank the team at One Management for their ongoing support and efforts.

Thanks to the family, community and friends who surround and encourage me constantly.

And thanks to my four boys, whose love is the centre of my life and the inspiration for everything I create.

For Mick.
Without you none of it is possible.

⌐⌐ hachette
   AUSTRALIA

Published in Australia and New Zealand in 2014
by Hachette Australia
(an imprint of Hachette Australia Pty Limited)
Level 17, 207 Kent Street, Sydney NSW 2000
www.hachette.com.au

10 9 8 7 6 5 4 3 2 1

Copyright © Julie Goodwin 2014

National Library of Australia
Cataloguing-in-Publication data:

  Goodwin, Julie, author.

  Julie Goodwin's 20/20 meals/Julie Goodwin.

  978 0 7336 3444 4 (paperback)

  Quick and easy cooking.

  641.555

Cover design and text design by Liz Seymour
Photography by Steve Brown
Food preparation by Tracey Meharg
Food styling by Trish Heagerty
Thanks to Howards Storage World www.hsw.com.au,
Le Creuset www.lecreuset.com.au, and GLAD Products www.glad.com.au
Typeset in 9/13 PMN Caecilia by Seymour Designs
Colour reproduction by Splitting Image
Printed in China by Toppan Leefung Printing Limited